THE WORD DWELLS AMONG US

The Word Dwells Among Us is one of the volumes in
a new series, IMPACT BOOKS, designed to bring the
modern reader the significant achievements of scholars, both
Catholic and non-Catholic, in the fields of Scripture, Theology, Philosophy, Mathematics, History, and the Physical and
Social Sciences. Among the titles in the series are:

The Word Dwells Among Us

A FOREWORD TO THE BIBLICAL BOOKS

by

WILLIAM E. LYNCH, C.M.

THE BRUCE PUBLISHING COMPANY
MILWAUKEE

IMPRIMI POTEST:

> JAMES A. FISCHER, C.M.
> *Provincial*
> Western Province Congregation of the Mission

NIHIL OBSTAT:

> FRANK J. MONTALBANO, O.M.I., S.S.L.
> *Censor deputatus*

IMPRIMATUR:

> ✠ ROBERT E. LUCEY
> *Archbishop of San Antonio*
> July 9, 1965

Library of Congress Catalog Card Number: 65–26692

© 1965 THE BRUCE PUBLISHING COMPANY
MADE IN THE UNITED STATES OF AMERICA

PREFACE

"LISTEN! A Sower went out to sow. The Sower sows the word. And there are those who hear the word and welcome it; and they bear fruit thirtyfold, sixtyfold, or a hundredfold" (Mk 4:3, 14, 20; translation of the *New English Bible*).

THE WORD DWELLS AMONG US introduces us to the word sown by God. Just as any seed, this word is not dead, but living and waiting fructification. God's word in the Bible awaits your reading to give you a hundredfold.

Your hundredfold is learning about God's love and His salvation. THE WORD DWELLS AMONG US consequently stresses the Bible's teaching.

God willed that His word be encased in enticing form. Hence this book seeks secondly to introduce you to the literary excellence of the Bible. The relation of archaeology, history, and science to the Bible will be discussed. Enough will be said to satisfy curiosity that God's word is historical.

The introduction attempts to show the dynamism of God's word as a living reality, a creative principle, which brings into being the book we call the Bible and the community to which this book preeminently belongs, the Church. A brief explanation will be given of such topics as the meaning of inspiration and the way to interpret the Bible. Without this information the reader of the Bible will never appreciate the riches and depths of God's word. Subsequent chapters will show God's word at work in history, first in the time of promise, the Old Testament, and then in the time of fulfillment, the New Testament.

I have endeavored in this book to present the findings of scholars in a popular way. The total absence of footnotes by no means implies that everything is original. Quite the contrary. In fact, I would like to thank all those scholars to whom I am deeply indebted. Especially to my Protestant friends am I grateful. They have become my friends, not in my meeting them, but in my spending many hours with their books, their thoughts.

I wish also to thank my personal friends. Originally, much of this book appeared as a commentary for sermons in the Archdiocese of San Antonio, Texas. The priests of the archdiocese and the faculty of its Assumption Seminary encouraged me to make the commentary into an introduction for the nonspecialist. THE WORD DWELLS AMONG US is the result. To name all of these friends would be tedious for the reader. To reward them by naming them would be belittling. "Your Father, who sees what is secret, will reward you" (Mt 6:4).

One last word on the mechanics of the book. Biblical quotations follow the Confraternity of Christian Doctrine translation for the Old Testament, except for the "historical books" (not yet completed in *CCD* version), where the Challoner-Rheims version has been used; and the Kleist-Lilly version of the New Testament. The spelling of biblical names and books is that commonly used in English — that of the Revised Standard Version.

"Listen! A Sower went out to sow . . ."

W. E. LYNCH, C.M.

BOOKS OF THE BIBLE AND THEIR ABBREVIATIONS

Old Testament

Gn	Genesis	Wis	Wisdom
Ex	Exodus	Sir	Sirach (Ecclesiasticus)
Lv	Leviticus		
Nm	Numbers	Is	Isaiah
Dt	Deuteronomy	Jer	Jeremiah
Jos	Joshua	Lam	Lamentations
Jgs	Judges	Bar	Baruch
Ru	Ruth	Ez	Ezekiel
1–2 Sm	1 and 2 Samuel	Dn	Daniel
1–2 Kgs	1 and 2 Kings	Hos	Hosea
1–2 Ch	1 and 2 Chronicles	Jl	Joel
Ezr	Ezra	Am	Amos
Neh	Nehemiah	Ob	Obadiah
Tb	Tobit	Jon	Jonah
Jdt	Judith	Mi	Micah
Est	Esther	Na	Nahum
Jb	Job	Hb	Habakkuk
Ps(s)	Psalms	Ze	Zephaniah
Prv	Proverbs	Hag	Haggai
Eccl	Ecclesiastes (Coheleth)	Zech	Zechariah
		Mal	Malachi
Ct	Canticle of Canticles	1–2 Mc	1 and 2 Maccabees

New Testament

Mt	Matthew	1–2 Thes	1 and 2 Thessalonians
Mk	Mark		
Lk	Luke	1–2 Tm	1 and 2 Timothy
Jn	Jn	Ti	Titus
Acts	The Acts of the Apostles	Phlm	Philemon
		Heb	Hebrews
Rom	Romans	Jas	James
1–2 Cor	1 and 2 Corinthians	1–2 Pt	1 and 2 Peter
Gal	Galatians	1–3 Jn	1, 2, and 3 John
Eph	Ephesians	Jude	Jude
Phil	Philippians	Ap	Apocalypse
Col	Colossians		

CONTENTS

PART TWO: THE NEW TESTAMENT

THE WORD DWELLS AMONG US

CHAPTER ONE

AN INTRODUCTORY WORD

God's Word and How to Interpret It

> All Scripture is inspired by God and useful for teaching, for reproving, for correcting, for instructing in holiness that the man of God may be perfect, equipped for every good deed (2 Tm 3:16 f.).

IN THIS sentence, St. Paul tells us that the Old Testament is useful for our perfection. And what he has to say applies to the New Testament as well, for the entire Bible is surely helpful for salvation. There we learn how an infinite and all-happy God stooped down to make pacts with finite man. In succeeding chapters, we shall explore the saving deeds of God recorded in the Bible.

The Bible, we say, is God's word. We put great stock in a word. We say, "I give you my word on this. . . ." "Oh, if only I hadn't said it. . . ." "Don't put that in writing." In the Bible God gives us His word. Thus it is in itself the most meaningful book that has ever been written for each of us individually and personally. It is God's word written for our perfection. God gave us His word on that.

Our purpose here is to understand what is meant by saying "the Bible is God's word," and how we must interpret this word and its message about the God of love. The final chapter of this book concludes by describing the efficacy of God's word.

1

What Is Inspiration?

To see why the Bible is God's word, it is necessary first to say something about inspiration, i.e., the divine guidance which results in the Bible's being God's word. To find out about inspiration we shall turn first to the popes, who, in their office as teachers of God's revealed word, have offered descriptions of inspiration. We shall then turn to scholars for the light they can throw on the human authors of the Bible and on the role that God plays in using these human authors as His helpers in writing the Bible. Finally, we shall conclude by seeing in what real way this book is God's word.

Perhaps one of the best ways to gain some idea of the meaning of inspiration is to take the popes as our guides, in particular, Popes Leo XIII and Benedict XV.

In his encyclical *Providentissimus Deus,* Pope Leo XIII offered an explanation of inspiration. According to Pope Leo:

> The Holy Spirit, by supernatural power, so moved and impelled them [the human authors of Scripture] to write — He was so present to them — that the things which He ordered, and those only, they first *rightly understood,* then *willed faithfully to write down,* and finally *expressed in apt words* and with infallible truth.

This statement of Pope Leo XIII is a very clear presentation of what the Church teaches about the inspiration of Sacred Scripture. What Pope Leo had to say was reiterated by Pope Benedict XV in his encyclical *Spiritus Paraclitus.* In that encyclical, the Roman Pontiff was expressly concerned with giving Catholics a good understanding of the Church's teaching on Scripture, in particular with regard to the interaction of God and man in writing the sacred books. Pope Benedict declared:

> He Himself [the Holy Spirit] so stirred and roused them [the human authors] by His supernatural power to write, and was so present to them in their writing that they *conceived rightly,* and *were minded to write faithfully,* and *expressed fittingly with unfailing truth,* all those things and those only which He bade them write.

If we reflect on these statements, we can soon conclude that the teaching authority of the Church includes three essential items in its conception of inspiration. The first requisite for inspiration is the action of God upon the *intellect* of the sacred writer; the second is His action upon his *will;* and the third is God's action upon the writer's *imaginative and literary faculties* throughout the entire composition of the book. The end of this activity is to express accurately everything God Himself wishes to be communicated, and those things only.

Recently scholars have been taking a very realistic approach to the authorship of the Bible. Most of us use various books before we write. We usually discuss our problems with friends. Then we sit down and write. Biblical scholars have seen that the books of the Bible are the result of such a procedure. The individual books, rather than being the product of merely an individual author, are the result of many people's work and rework. In fact, the biblical books came from a community of people: in the Old Testament, Israel; in the New, the Church.

Sitting around the campsite at night, the people would discuss a kernel of truth about God, would penetrate more profoundly into the truth, and would make new judgments on it. When we discuss the various books of the Bible, we shall see indications of this group collaboration, especially in Genesis and the Gospels.

The Bible is thus the effect of the entire community's activity. Where does the supernatural power of inspiration, of which Pope Leo was talking, enter? Is he not talking only about an individual? How is this activity pertinent to a community?

We believe that Pope Pius XII in his encyclical on the Mystical Body has given the principle which explains this apparent dilemma. He calls the Holy Spirit the Soul of the Church. The human soul makes the body human and is the source for the activity proper to each part of the body. For

example, the hand is both human and able to write because
of the soul. Similarly, the Holy Spirit acts in each individual
of the community known as the people of God, making him
a member of the community and enabling him to do his task
as a member of God's people. The authors of the Bible are
both part of the community and inspired writers because of
the Holy Spirit, who was the moving power behind the Israelite community in the Old Testament and the "Comforter"
promised by Jesus to His Church in the New Testament.

Precisely what effect does the Spirit have when influencing
the individual? Since both St. Luke (1:1–4) and the author
of 2 Maccabees (2:24 ff.) say that they worked for their
knowledge, it is evident that knowledge was not simply given
to them. When, however, they came to a conclusion about
their knowledge, God's Spirit was inspiring. He moved them
to say that this was true or not. When the individual judged,
God judged. Since these writers were men, they had to express
their judgments in words and figure; they had to communicate what they had experienced in a human mode. In short,
they had to use words and literary imagination. And the
Spirit guided them in all this work, so that their word would
be God's word.

Summarizing what has been said about inspiration, we
see the following. Inspiration is the activity of the Spirit,
acting as the Soul of the community, the Shaper of God's
people. The Bible is the result of the Community's activity.
The inspired individuals judge with God's judgment. The
words to which they bear witness are uttered under God's
inspiring activity. The biblical word is God's word. It is His
word for our perfection.

What the author meant, God meant. It follows from this
that there can be no mistake in the Bible. The Bible is the
unique book that is inerrant. It is errorless in the sense, however, in which the authors meant it. We now turn to the
principles for interpreting the Bible, God's word.

The Teaching of the Church and Biblical Interpretation

The Church's teaching is found most solemnly in the bishops of the world gathered together for a Council and in the pope speaking authoritatively and in the full exercise of his office. As far as expressing the mind of the Church on scriptural passages is concerned, however, neither Councils nor popes have defined a great deal. *Some* scriptural texts have been the subject of conciliar or papal definition, and a listing of some of these may be instructive: Romans 5:12, original sin (DB, #791); John 3:5, baptism (DB, #858); Matthew 26:26, the Eucharist (DB, #874); Luke 22:19 and parallels, the priesthood (DB, #949); John 20:22, penance (DB, #913); Matthew 16:18, the papacy (DB, #1833).

Pius XII has summed up the matter of the Church's authoritative interpretation, "In the immense matter contained in the Sacred Books . . . there are but few texts whose sense has been defined by the authority of the Church nor are those more numerous about which the teaching of the Holy Fathers is unanimous" (*Divino Afflante Spiritu*, #47). It is evident that no interpretation may be propounded which would contradict any dogma of the faith. The Church always claims, as custodian of revelation, the right to interpret the Bible.

In 1902, the Church set up a Commission to safeguard the Bible. The Biblical Commission was not meant to define texts, but to indicate prudent interpretations. This Commission is still in operation and the decrees which it issues are intended to aid Catholic scholars in interpreting the Bible. The Biblical Commission, which ordinarily manifests an attitude of caution, has permitted some of its decrees to fall into disuse. Thus, Father Wikenhauser in his commentary has published without ecclesiastical censure a date for St. Luke's Gospel which differs from that taught by the Commission (A. Wikenhauser, *New Testament Introduction* [Herder and Herder, 1960], pp. 200 and 221). This is but one of the many possible examples in Catholic books. Of course, care must be taken; willing submission to the Holy See is always implied.

The Church is the ultimate judge of the meaning of the Bible. However, as we have seen, she has explicitly interpreted only a very few texts, and implicitly not too many more. How, then, are we to understand the rest of the Bible (and remember, this means most of the biblical texts)? To the literary principles answering this query, we now turn.

The Scientific Interpretation of the Bible

A science called "hermeneutics" has arisen to give principles of understanding the Bible. It is as valid as the research and logic that go into it. It is as limited as the human who researches and concludes. Hermeneutics seeks the meaning of the word, the context, the author, the date, the environment, and the type of literature.

What is the meaning of a word? Although it is difficult at times to determine the precise meaning of many biblical passages, we can be guided by the firmly rooted conclusion of modern biblical scholarship. Today scholars, in general, distinguish four major senses, four aspects under which the words of the Bible can be understood. The meaning can be considered as that given by: (1) both God and man; (2) God; (3) theologians; (4) preachers. The meaning intended by both God and man is called the *literal* sense. If the meaning is intended by God, it is called the spiritual sense and occurs in things, or people, or events (called the typical sense) and in words (the fuller sense). Theologians can draw conclusions from the Bible that are not strictly the meaning originally intended by the biblical writers. This is called the theological sense. Lastly, anyone can accommodate Scripture to his own usage. Pius XII commends prudence in the use of Scripture in this way.

Thus there are four biblical senses: sense *of* the Bible, the literal sense; sense *in* the Bible, spiritual sense; sense *out of* the Bible, theological sense; and lastly, sense *into* the Bible, the accommodation. There is as yet no consistency in the use of this terminology, so take care when reading other authors not to be led astray by terminology.

What then, to return to the original question, is the meaning of a word? For the most part, we will be interested only in the literal sense. Thanks to the labor of dedicated scholars over the centuries, dictionaries are at hand to tell the meaning of words. Yet disagreements still exist, and certain variations of translation do and will always occur.

After the meaning of the word under consideration is determined, the context must be considered. The context means that which goes before and comes after the word. As anyone knows, you can prove almost anything from the Bible if the verse is taken out of its context. For instance, we can show that suicide is a good thing by citing Matthew 27:5, "Judas went away and hanged himself," and joining this to Luke 10:37, "Model your conduct on his." Thus, one should hang himself. But no one would accuse Matthew or Luke of teaching suicide simply because that is not what they meant in context.

One of the most important aspects of modern biblical studies is the study of literary form, although this facet has, at times, been magnified too greatly. Far from being novel or arbitrary, the literary form is an ordinary and inescapable part of every piece of literature and the analysis of it. By definition, a literary form (genre, type) is a mold of writing, a "pigeonhole" of an idea. Some biblical examples are familiar to us, e.g., a letter, a parable, a fable. Some biblical examples are unfamiliar, as, for example "midrash" and "myth."

As noted, these literary forms are inescapable to every piece of writing. When you wish to write a letter, you're using the literary mold of "letter." This is simply the type by which we've agreed to prolong a conversation or carry on business with one another. The literary form is not some *Deus ex*

machina invented by exegetes to worm their way out of difficulties. The biblical author, as all writers, has expressed
himself in these categories of writing. He did so more or less
unconsciously, somewhat as we do when we choose to write
a personal note. A letter is the way to do it, so the literary
form of letter is the form we unconsciously select.

Another literary category in the Bible is the parable. Our
Lord Himself was an expert at using this plausible story
which teaches one and only one lesson. An allegory is similar
to a parable in that it is a plausible story. Unlike the parable,
however, the allegory teaches many lessons through the symbols of the story. Thus Isaiah 5:1-5 teaches through the
allegory of the vineyard that God, who has loved Israel and
tenderly cared for it, must destroy Israel for its own good,
inasmuch as Israel has rejected His care.

The Old Testament has a fable not unlike those of Aesop.
This is illustrated in Judges 9:8-15, where we find a fictitious
and implausible narrative about talking trees whose purpose
is to teach that the Shechemites chose the worst possible one
to be king.

We are accustomed to these literary forms. Letters and
fables and allegories are still used today. Among ourselves
there are some strange literary forms in existence. A doctor's
prescription makes no sense to us laymen, but it does to the
pharmacist. But that's their way of communicating together.
So, too, the biblical authors, in addition to using parables,
fables, and allegories, have some ways of writing that are
somewhat strange to us.

Pius XII said that we should not be surprised at this. He
wrote, "For the ancient peoples of the East, in order to express
their ideas, did not always employ those forms or kinds of
speech, which we use today . . . [They used] customary modes
of expression and narration peculiar to the ancients, which
used to be employed in the mutual dealings of social life
and which in fact were sanctioned by common usage" (*Divino
Afflante Spiritu*, # #36 and 38).

St. Paul uses one of these unfamiliar literary forms to teach in 1 Corinthians, "Why, it is written in the Law of Moses, 'you shall not muzzle the ox when it threshes the grain.' Is God's concern for the oxen? Or does he say this especially for our benefit? It is written, of course, for our benefit, because the plowman should plow with hope and the thresher should thresh with hope of a share in the crop. If we have sown spiritual seed, is it too much if we reap a material harvest?" (9:9–11). If you look up the quotation from the Law of Moses (Dt 25:4), you will see that the quote does indeed apply to an ox, teaching that a master should not be too harsh on his animals.

St. Paul, however, draws a new teaching out of this quotation, applying it to the teachers of the Christian Gospel: they too deserve to be fed. This "drawing out" is a common way that the teachers of Paul's day had of bringing out new ideas from the Old Testament. It was so common that it had a name, "midrash." Other examples can be found in Scripture too, and we shall return to the midrash when studying the New Testament (pp. 121–123).

Paul's meditation on the Old Testament to develop a different insight or meaning is not really too unfamiliar to us. The preacher who applies the Gospel to our own situation is doing something along the same lines.

Another type of literary form that raises eyebrows is that of myth. By myth we do not mean a story about gods nor a make-believe. We mean, rather, that literary form which tries to explain the present world through God's act of creation. As God once did, so He is now doing! God created and maintains His creation. Psalm 73:12 f., for instance, states, "O God . . . you doer of saving deeds on earth. . . . You smashed the heads of the dragons in the waters." The dragon was a mythological monster of primeval times according to the peoples of the ancient Near East, and the Hebrews, remember, were one of these peoples. God, according to the myth, overcame this dragon. God was powerful

enough to create despite the limitation of the creature, so the
Psalmist teaches — through a myth. Moreover, He continues
creation — the first act of salvation (cf. p. 23) — in His
present saving deeds. Philosophers would rather say that
God's activity maintains the creature in its very being. The
Psalmist puts the same reality in mythological language,
"God, doer of saving deeds. You smashed the heads of the
dragon." Both ways of expressing reality are valid. And perhaps for our age of science fiction which seeks its god in
science, the biblical author's point of view is much more
understandable than that of the philosopher. This is not
meant as any condemnation or criticism of science or philosophy. It is just a plea that the Bible, with its mythological
expressions of reality, be given a chance to explain in its
own language the reality for which scientists grope.

And since we've brought up the matter of science, here's
a practical application of these literary forms in regard to
areas of possible conflict between science and the Bible —
the Bible and modern science do collide head-on at times,
or at least seem to. Thus Genesis 1:1–2:4a says that creation
took place in six days. Modern science disagrees, explaining
that the years of creation are almost incalculably high. Who
is right? Again, Joshua 10:13 says, "And the sun stood still."
Modern science knows that it is the earth that is moving.
For the earth to stand still and not have all the inhabitants
pitched out into outer space and the rest of the planets thrown
off their gravitational spin would demand a colossal number
of miracles. Is the Bible or science right?

The answer, of course, is that both are right. There is
only an apparent conflict here. Remember, the purpose of
the Bible in general is to teach a religious truth. Who would
accuse a man who said, "I was up with the sunrise this
morning," of error when he wanted to say how early he
arose? Neither should we accuse the Bible of scientific error
since it is not teaching science. Genesis 1:1–2:4a *teaches*
that God is the perfect Workman by saying that God worked

six days and rested on the seventh. Surely, you and I don't use the "week" to mean a "perfect workman," but then perhaps the Jew for whom this passage was originally written would not have understood our use of "a million and one things to do this morning." Every language and every people have their own proper way of expressing ideas. The same is true for Joshua 10:13; this verse is a part of a popular song and should be permitted all the embellishments of our modern ballads with no accusation of scientific error. When discussing the Books of Genesis and Judges, we will return to these two perennially vexing problems (pp. 21 f. and 48).

Besides the word, context, and literary form, it is helpful to know the date and audience in order to ascertain the meaning of Scripture. The bulk of this book examines the details of these problems. Here we wish only to set down the principles of interpretation.

A word of caution in all this. By detailing the obvious, we might be instilling in readers a fear of reading the Bible. Right from the beginning, let us realize that anyone reading the Bible will understand a great deal of it. However, if we take time to apply the literary rules to the Bible, our understanding will be much better. We all experience the same in whatever we read. Anyone can profit from Shakespeare's *Merchant of Venice*. But if we know that Shakespeare was English, writing in the seventeenth century when the Jews were greatly despised, we realize the irony of the close victory, yet ultimate defeat of Portia's enemy.

Keep in mind the fact that most of the Bible must be interpreted according to the human science of hermeneutics. Then the seeming capriciousness of the Bible's professional interpreters, who are called exegetes, should be less scandalous. Human beings, using a human science, they must be constantly learning more; they will often disagree among themselves. Just as we learn more about the Word become flesh by studying more theology, so too the exegete learns more about God's word in ink by studying more about the Bible.

PART ONE: THE OLD TESTAMENT

CHAPTER TWO

THE CREATING WORD (Genesis 1–3)

THE BIBLE starts in with the very beginning of things. "In the beginning God created the heavens and the earth." With the strokes of a master, Genesis depicts God as the unique Creator of all things. Lord above all creatures, God has made man to the level of a master also. Not content with leaving man as a created lord, God raised him to the supernatural plane, to life with Himself. Happy with God and his fellow creatures, man nevertheless sinned. God, forced to punish man, promised to aid him.

The teachings of the first three chapters of the Bible are thus summarized: God, the Creator of all, puts man on a plane with Himself. Man refuses to remain there. Sin, suffering, and death begin. But man lives in hope.

The compiler of Genesis 1–3 is answering the most asked of all questions. "Who is God?" "Who is man?" "Whence come the sun, moon, trees?" "Why are there male and female?" "What causes sin?" "Why is there suffering?"

The man of faith reads deeply into these chapters and comes out with eternal answers. "Who is God?" The absolute Creator whose act and words cause to be that which, one second before, was not — this is God. "In the beginning God created the heavens and the earth." "God said 'Let there be light' and there was light" (Gn 1:1, 3). All things are created by God. The sun and moon, the day and the night are no gods. They depend on the One God who was before them and at whose word they all came to be.

This then is "Who is God": the omnipotent Creator who made all things very good (Gn 1:31), and changed chaos into cosmos. But we said before that these chapters also answered the question, "Who is man?" At the pinnacle of God's visible creation stand the two sexes, "male and female he created them" (Gn 1:27). Of all creatures, the only one about whom the author makes God deliberate — "let us make" — is man. Of all creatures, the only one made like to God — "in our image and likeness" (Gn 1:26) — is man. God gave man dominion over all His creatures (Gn 1:28). This is the sublime and unique dignity of the human: (1) to be like God; (2) to be the apex of God's visible creatures; (3) to be a ruler.

Genesis' teachings proceed. Not all the questions asked have been solved so far. We know now who God is and what man is. Humans wish to know the answers to other fundamental questions, such as, "If God is good, why is there suffering?" "What is sin?" "What is sanctifying grace?" "Is a woman not so beneath man that he may have two wives just as he can have two chairs?"

Biblical scholars distinguish two accounts of creation in Genesis. In the first of these (Gn 1:1–2:4a) man was the highest of God's visible creation. The second account (Gn 2:4b–3:24) tells that God raised him to His own friendship. God, after creating man (Gn 2:7), put him into a garden in Eden, a place of bliss (Gn 2:8), where it was God's custom to walk with man (Gn 3:8). This garden was altogether special, particularly to a desert Israelite. It had so much water that its superabundance was enough for the rest of the rivers of the world (Gn 2:10–14). The garden had food in abundance. Thus did the biblical writer describe God's friendship and blessings in a very simple way. Today, in our advanced revelation, we would call these things God's graces and gifts. Does our technical language describe the reality nearly so well as the poetic, simple terms of Genesis, "The Lord walked in the garden in the cool of evening" (Gn 3:8), "The Lord God planted a garden in Eden and put there the man he had formed" (Gn 2:8)?

Genesis' images tell the reality of man's creation and elevation to friendship with God. They tell too that man could be immortal, since the tree of life was provided for him (Gn 2:9). Man was innocent; in the face of nakedness, no feeling of shame was present (Gn 2:25). You see, God had made for this man a fit helper; the sovereign man had the right to name all the creatures that God made for him (Gn 2:20), but none was a helper fit for him. Thus God made a second human of the same nature as man. The image of woman coming from man's own matter well figures the nature common to both (Gn 2:22).

Woman too, so Genesis teaches, is dependent on man since she comes from him, is meant to be his helper, and is named by him. The strong tendency which man has for woman and vice versa is God-given since God made them to complement one another — He made them for each other. At the same time, however, man must cling to a unique partner no matter how unending, unbreakable, or intimate may be his other ties (Gn 2:24). "Consequently, what God has yoked together, man may not separate" (Mt 19:6). With this, some more queries are answered. We know now that grace is friendship with God; that man was originally happy; and that man and his helpmate were to continue living forever in their God-given friendship.

Man and woman were to live forever in their supernatural happiness — provided they obeyed God's single command. The figures of the trees, snake, and fruit need detailed treatment and we will leave this until we have seen the literary forms of the chapters (cf. p. 20 f.).

Chapter 3 details that man did not remain happy. An alluring temptation occasions sin, and immediately everything is changed. Shame of their own bodies replaces the original innocence of man and woman. Before, they were friends of God; now they hide, fearful of Him (Gn 3:1–11).

What is left for God except to punish? The tempter is immediately sentenced without opportunity to gainsay his own guilt (Gn 3:14). Woman, continuing to desire man,

will suffer in the term of her desire: childbirth (Gn 3:16).
Man, the sovereign of all things, will be made to suffer by
the lowest of things, the earth itself. And the ultimate destiny
will be not immortality, but death, and then dust (Gn 3:17–
19). Man has lost God's friendship, God's blessings, and is
destitute. Sin, suffering, and death have begun.

What hope, what reason for living then is left for man?
God is good. In the very first act of condemnation God tells
man that ultimate victory is to be his (Gn 3:15). Man's
seed will one day conquer the tempter. Later revelation clari-
fies the characters in this scene: the woman: Mary; the snake:
Satan; the man's seed: Christ and the Mystical Body.

The man of faith now knows many answers. What is grace?
It is friendship with God, walking and talking with God and
living in God's garden. "With God," this is the simple answer
of what is grace. Why do I suffer, if God is good? Man,
raised by God to a state where he could have been happy
forever, refused obedience and wished to become independent
of God. God punished him by making man dependent on
creatures and experiencing suffering.

In three chapters of alluring charm, the Bible describes
God as the Creator who chose man, above all the creatures,
to be His friend. Man, instead of keeping his original dominion over all the creatures and his orginal state of innocence, chose to sin. Suffering and death resulted.

What is the literary framework in which these teachings
are encased? As noted already, we are taking for granted the
strong hypothesis that scholars make for two separate accounts in these three chapters. In so doing, we are following
Pius XII's injunction of 1943, "Moreover we may rightly
and deservedly hope that our times also can contribute something towards the deeper and more accurate interpretation
of Sacred Scripture. For not a few things, especially in matters
pertaining to history, were scarcely at all or not fully explained by the commentators of past ages, since they lacked
almost all the information which was needed for their clearer

exposition. How difficult for the Fathers themselves, and indeed well nigh unintelligible were certain passages is shown, among other things, by the oft-repeated efforts of many of them to explain the first chapters of Genesis" (*Divino Afflante Spiritu*, #31). After decades of research, Catholic and non-Catholic scholars in general accept that many preexisting documents were spliced together to form Genesis. This multiple source explanation is a scholarly hypothesis — about as certain as the atomic theory of matter.

The first account (Gn 1:1–2:4a) comes from what is called the "priestly" source, dated about 500 B.C. This document runs all through the first five Books of the Bible and is probably greatly influenced by the priests and levites. The second account (Gn 2:4b–3:24) is from what is called the "Yahwist" source, dated c. 900 B.C.; its name comes from the propensity of its compiler to use the name "Yahweh" (Appendix I) instead of "Elohim" for God. Each of these sources and at least two others can be determined by the style, vocabulary, and predominating interest. Suffice it to say that Catholic and other scholars grant sources for the Bible with no difficulty. It is a working hypothesis that in no way militates against inspiration or inerrancy and does clarify many difficulties.

Each source, as we said, describes things in its own way. The first account is an almost direct religious teaching: In the beginning God created the universe. Not so the second. Filled with imagery, its figures are its didactic vehicle. Anthropomorphic in every description, its choice of describing man's creation is, "Then the Lord God formed man out of the dust of the ground and breathed into his nostrils the breath of life, and man became a living being" (Gn 2:7). Each document has its own beauty, and each must be understood in its own right. One is almost direct theological teaching. The other instructs in religion through figures.

What is the literary form of each source? This has already been suggested. Genesis 1:1–2:4a is priestly doctrine — revelation which the priests taught and handed down for centuries. Genesis 2:4b–3:24, as the Biblical Commission says, is "popular description." As a "popular description," God's walking and talking with man were most expressive figures of God's friendship — now we call it sanctifying grace — but, for all that, a figure. What difference does it make if man did not eat an apple, so long as the truth is present? Man sinned by disobeying God. Did you feel a little flush come to your face when it was said, "What difference does it make if man did not eat an apple?" You should not have, you know. Look high and low in the text. There is no mention of an apple. Of fruit, yes, but of an apple, no! What we are driving is that the sin of disobedience remains whether the apple is removed or whether we say that the fruit is a figure of some specifically unknown act of disobedience.

There are many figures in Chapters 2 and 3. The serpent and the tree of the knowledge of good and evil are among the most perplexing. All of these figures are based on thinking and imagery contemporary with the author. The serpent is a figure of a magic power for cunning, sensuality, and healing; it is, in other words, a figure of intellectual and physical life. The tree of the knowledge of good and evil is probably a figure not of omniscience, but of sexual potency whose fruit was an extraordinary aphrodisiac.

Knowing the significance of these figures, we can put the whole picture of Genesis 3 into more modern language. Remember that all we are describing is the *picture,* not the teaching. According to the picture, the myth, God had promised man personal immortality (tree of life). But God had likewise commanded man to refrain from immortality through having children (tree of knowledge of good and evil). (Here it is pertinent to note that the Semite had no notion of life after death until a century or so before Christ. His life continued in his children.) Some temptation (the walking serpent) to life through procreation induced the woman to tempt the man to follow her in eating the aphrodisiac (fruit of the tree of the knowledge of good and evil). The punishment for disobedience repays the sin. The high-strutting tempter is degraded (the walking snake made to grovel). Sex is a constant war which mankind will ultimately overcome (3:15). Woman, who tempted man to live in his children, will suffer in her longings for him and in the term of her longing (pain in childbirth and in her husband's dominion of her). Man willed to live forever, the way he wanted, not the way God wanted. He will live a dying life and terminate in death (sweat of your brow and dust). Man got what he chose: a life in his children instead of personal immortality.

The author did not make up these figures, these pictures. They already existed at the time Genesis was compiled. Childbirth pained. Man's toil was frustrating. People died. Slowly the realization of the dissatisfaction with "this life only in view" was coming. The snake was an accepted superstitious symbol imparting life. The knowledge of good and evil meant to become sexually potent.

The author did not teach that sexual intercourse was wrong any more than he taught that a snake once walked. He did not teach that the originating sin was one of sex, any more than he taught that God had feet to walk in Eden. The author did not teach that mankind would not have reproduced had they not sinned, any more than he taught that God was a potter who shaped mankind.

As we have seen, he did teach that after God had created and raised man to His friendship, man sinned. The author taught that suffering came because of man, not God. He taught that man died because of man's sin. He taught that God promised help to man. He taught it all in an unforgettable, even though temporally conditioned, story.

As said, these three chapters are of the literary forms of "sacred doctrine" and "popular description." Thus they teach no empiriological science. Instructing in religion, the author had no interest in and no knowledge (it seems safe to say) of whether creation took place in six days or 600,000,000 years. The word "day" teaches the doctrine that creation was done by God in time and refers not at all to a geological age. The seven days of the creation-teaching give the biblically perfect week: six days of work and one of rest. They teach God as the perfect Workman. Genesis simply taught by this figure that God was the perfect Creator. As far as all this goes too, there is no use asking Genesis if man's body evolved from the ape; Genesis used in a popular description the figure of dust to say that God created man. There is no astronomy, geology, biology, or paleontology taught in the description by figures and appearances in Genesis.

With this brief theological explanation and statement of literary form, let it not be thought that all has been said about the first three chapters of Genesis. Of all the Bible, the first eleven chapters, which deal with man from creation to the time of Abraham, are perhaps the most difficult. To understand them properly, something should be said, for instance, about the Semitic cosmogony of waters over a vault in which the stars are fastened. Otherwise the story of Noah makes little sense. Under the vault is earth and under the earth is more water. For a proper appreciation of the advanced and unique theology of these chapters, something should also be said about their contemporaneous myths, to which Genesis has some external resemblances — those of Babylon and Phoenicia at least. And lastly, for a truer presentation of these chapters, mention should be made of the irony of the phrase in 3:12, "The woman you placed at my side" and the half-truth of "You shall not eat of any tree of the garden" in 3:2.

You probably noted with some consternation that neither the name "Adam" nor "Eve" appeared in these pages. These individuals did not appear in Genesis 1–3 either. Adam as an individual probably appears for the first time only in Genesis 4:1. "Adam" is a transliteration of a Hebrew word which means "man." "Eve" is a Latin transliteration of the

Hebrew meaning "living one." It cannot be shown that
Genesis teaches the creation of only one man and one woman,
though it does teach, as we shall later see (p. 26) that all
humans come from one pair. Call that pair "Adam" and
"Eve" if you want. It is certain that they would not mind
after all these years, and besides that, these are rather fitting
names for "The Man" and "The Living One."

The above is in keeping with Pius XII's *Humani Generis:*

> The faithful cannot embrace that opinion called "polygenism"
> which maintains either that after Adam there existed on this earth
> true men who did not take their origin through natural generation
> from him as from the first parent of all, or that Adam represents
> a certain number of first parents, because it is in no way apparent
> how such an opinion can be reconciled with that which the Church
> proposes with regard to original sin, which proceeds from a sin
> actually committed by an individual Adam and which through
> generation is passed on to all and is in everyone as his own
> (*Enchiridion Biblicum*, 1954, #617).

Let it not be imagined that all the difficulties of Genesis
1–3 are now resolved. The translations "mist" in Genesis
2:6 and "crush" in 3:15 are not certain. There are some
forty interpretations of "image and likeness" of 1:26. Not
all agree on our picture of the symbols in Genesis 3.

After discussing the literary, scientific, and unsolved problems of Genesis 1–3, let us return to its theological teachings.
As we said in the very first pages of this book, the theme of
the Bible is God's love as epitomized in His covenant with
Israel. God chose Israel because mankind sinned. Creation is
for salvation. Sin in Israel is not scandalous; from the beginning it had ever been thus. The God of the Exodus who freed
His people from slavery was the God who was above all
gods, the Creator who was in the beginning. Israel's primeval
account of creation was in keeping with its knowledge of its
faithful, omnipotent God and its disloyal, weak fellowman.
Israel did look toward the day when man's seed would crush
the tempter. We Christians know He has come in our Messiah, but we know only because the Word dwelt among us.

THE WORD UNHEEDED

Sin's Wake (Genesis 4–11)

As WE have said before, the Bible deals with the most absorbing questions of human existence. In this chapter we shall see that original sin is found in the descendants of Adam. Man sins ever more grievously against God. God punishes mankind. Finally, in the midst of all the world's sin, God chose for Himself the father of His chosen people.

These thoughts are deep. Thank God that the author of Genesis presents them in a simple, storylike manner. This is the way he chose to teach God's mercy in the midst of man's sin; God's choice of a special people; man's unity from Adam; and man's tendency to sin after the originating sin.

We shall consider Genesis 4–11 in the following order: teaching, literary sources and forms, and last, questions raised by science and history. In simple language, the biblical redactor has taught mankind's sin and God's punishment. Genesis tells us that we tend to sin since that has been the way of Adam's descendants ever since Adam. There was first of all Cain who slew his own blood brother, because Abel, his brother, offered a sacrifice pleasing to God (Gn 4:1–16). Lamech followed Cain and bettered him: Lamech was so cruel that he boasted, "I kill a man for wounding me, a youth for bruising me." He was so much worse than the unrepentant brother-killer Cain that he avenged himself seventy times more: "If Cain shall be avenged sevenfold, Lamech seventy times sevenfold" (Gn 4:23 f.). Cain and Lamech show that sin followed Adam's sin and increased. The genealogy of Chapter 5 has for its theological purpose

24

to tell the same story of sin. The decreasing ages bespeak an increase of sin and, hence, decreased longevity. Adam lived to 930; the last in the series to 777. Man was wandering farther and farther from the Giver of life (for more on the genealogy, cf. p. 28 f.).

The wake of Adam's voyage from Eden becomes even more destructive. As Genesis 6:5 expressed it, "man's every thought and all the inclinations of his heart were only evil." This judgment on all of mankind was made after the affair between the daughters of men and the sons of God (cf. p. 30). This union was sinful, based solely on naturalistic, sensual allurement; the judgment that the "wickedness of man on the earth was great" results from this union. Adam's sin increased in Cain, worsened again in Lamech, and reached the stage of enveloping all mankind in its heinousness.

One more account of mankind's general sinfulness will set the immediate stage of Abraham's choice by God. Man plans to build himself a tower and a city lest "we be scattered all over the earth" (Gn 11:4) in defiant disobedience to God's command to "fill the earth" (Gn 9:1). Again mankind turned against God. Would God liquidate His disloyal humanity?

We shall turn in a minute to this question. The compiler of Genesis has taught many things while relating man's iniquities. For our consideration the most important lesson is that Adam's descendants sinned; we call this tendency to sin "original sin." The author narrated the fact of original sin without giving it this name and without describing the causal link between Adam's and Cain's and Lamech's sin and ours, but he did teach original sin in act.

Man sins. Is God merciful or vengeful? Again we turn to the Bible to see what the truth of the matter is. God, for His own reasons, is merciful to sinning man. His first mercy was shown to mankind (cf. p. 18). Cain also receives God's mercy in the mysterious words of Genesis 4:15, "Whoever kills Cain shall be punished sevenfold. Then the Lord gave Cain a token so that no one finding him should kill him." Mankind, sinful to the extent that we have seen described — "man's every thought and all the inclinations of his heart were only evil" (Gn 6:5) — was punished with the Flood. But God was merciful to mankind by saving Noah and indeed telling Noah, God's new creation, "Be fruitful, multiply, and fill the earth" (Gn 9:1). Not only did God save mankind from total destruction, but blessed it in order to procreate. And even when mankind banded together to thwart God's command to procreate as described in the Tower of Babel, God chose one man for all: "All the nations of the earth shall be blessed" (Gn 12:3).

The story of Genesis 4–11 is one which tells God's mercy and man's sin. It is an unpleasant, though true, account of the result of Adam's sin. Intermingled with this, the chief theological doctrine of these chapters, are many other teachings. Two of them are important and not immediately evident, namely: the unity of the whole human race from Adam, and the direct ratio between sin and culture.

As we mentioned on page 23, Pius XII in his encyclical *Humani Generis* teaches that all mankind now comes from Adam. The Bible in its own way teaches this same unity. The genealogical table of Genesis 5 brings mankind from Adam to Noah. Chapters 10 and 11 theologically make all mankind descend from Noah. This is in keeping with the Church's teaching on original sin's coming from Adam. As St. Paul says, "Therefore, as through one man sin entered into the world and through sin death, and thus death has passed unto all men because all have sinned" (Rom 5:12). And who is to say that Paul did not have in mind the decreasing ages of the men of the genealogy of Genesis 5?

Genesis 4–11 are filled with theological import. Man's sin and God's mercy, the unity of the human race from Adam. Another implicit teaching is that of cultural, of material advancement, which goes hand in glove with sin — or would Genesis' author have put it vice versa? As two noted Protestant scholars put it:

Man's civilized life advances by successive stages, and his progress in the arts of civilization corresponds with the increasing complexity of his sin. The first clothes (3:7–21) and the cultivation of the soil are associated with the fall of man from his created state. Cain the murderer is associated with Cain the builder of the first city (4:17). Progress in the arts of nomadic life, metallurgy, and music culminate in the completely hardened and vengeful Lamech (verses 18–24). With the establishment of grape or vineyard culture we are presented with the picture of a good man drunk (Gen. 9:20 f.). The growth and separation of nations and languages is associated with the story of the Tower of Babel (11:1–9). In this interpretation, then, the growth of civilization is accompanied by a degeneration of the spirit of man, caused by the human refusal to accept all the conditions of creation" (Wright and Fuller, *The Book of the Acts of God* [New York: Doubleday Anchor Books, 1960], p. 60).

So much for the theological teaching of these chapters. What about the sources? Are they also determined by scholars for these chapters? Probably some of them already became quite evident to you. Yes, the so-called Priestly compiler (cf. p. 19) is at work especially in Chapter 5. Both he and the Yahwist source (cf. p. 19) have side-by-side accounts of the Flood in Genesis 6–8. As far as that goes, the rest of the chapters can be parceled out, by strict principles based on vocabulary, style, accent of interest, between both Priestly and Yahwist.

Of course, the authors used literary forms. Genesis 4:1–16 seems to interweave a ritualistic sacrifice and stories explaining the origin of the vendetta and the feud between the nomad and the agriculturist. With these stories, the author had drawn a picture of the first act after originating sin. It is the gross sin of ritual fratricide. Its punishment is fruitless toil and banishment to a land where no cult of the Lord is known. The teaching conveyed through these stories, we have already noted: man sins after the originating sin.

Genesis 4:17–23 is a genealogy. It comes from a different source but parallels the teaching of the genealogy of Genesis 5. Another genealogy is found in Chapter 11. "Genealogy" as a literary form is strange to us, but not to the people of the times. In fact, in some accounts, Babylonians lived to be more than 20,000 years old and one of them hit 72,000 years. Neither the biblical redactor nor the Babylonian composer were trying to give the ages of their ancestors. Genesis' genealogies teach through the picture of life's shortening that sin is increasing.

Chapters 6–8 contain two meshed accounts of the Flood. We will never know if seven pairs or two animals went into the ark. We will never know if the Flood lasted forty days and nights or one hundred and fifty. Can we be certain that there was a Flood? From the almost universal and seemingly primitive echoes of something like a huge flood found in the traditions of many peoples, it seems that a great flood did occur. Remember though, whether historical or not, the teaching of the Flood about God's punishment for sin and God's mercy is true and certain.

Chapter 10 is a unique genealogy, called the Table of the Nations. It probably relies on a tenth-century B.C. tradition. Israel grouped persons, countries, cities, peoples, and tribes together. The basis of the division is friendship with Israel. If the group was Israel's friend, it was descended from Shem or Japheth. If enemies, the group was descended from the cursed Ham. Friendship, not ethnic relationship, nor racial similarity, is the principle of division. The teaching is that all come from God and all come from one man.

Chapter 11 after verse 10 is a genealogy, teaching the increase of sin and preparation for Abraham. Verses 1 to 9 recount the famous Tower of Babel. There are really two stories here. One tells how mankind built a tower to make a name for itself. The second depicts mankind's building a city not to be separated. The teaching of each is simple enough: mankind sins after the Flood.

These eight chapters teach sin's increase after the originating sin. The teaching is enclosed interestingly in genealogies, current stories of blood feuds, ritualistic sacrifices, the Flood, the unique city, and the Tower of Babel.

The Bible is not teaching anything about the ages of these men. We are still not certain precisely what the ages mean. The teaching that men's lives were shortened as they sinned more seems to be a good conclusion, but it is theological and not in any way at variance with the anthropologists. Genesis is teaching religion through genealogical tables; it is as interesting as teaching it according to many a catechism. If the scientist insists that men of yore lived less than the years ascribed in Genesis, more power to him. We have no quarrel.

If the ages of the Genesis account do not come at odds with anthropology, surely the extent of the Flood does. Or does it? Natural historians would argue that the ark could never have housed the 510,000 distinct species of living creatures. They say that the amount of water needed to flood the entire earth would have been so stupendous as to be inconceivable. But the Bible is not teaching the history of the Flood. If mankind has in its traditions the existence of a great deluge, that conclusion is for archaeologists and historians to settle. The Bible uses contemporary stories of a flood to teach God's justice and God's mercy.

Neither is the Bible's teaching that man's languages became diverse at the Tower of Babel. Again, the literary form of an age-old story is used to teach man's sinfulness. Last, it follows that neither the Table of Nations in Genesis 10 nor the curse of Canaan in Genesis 9:25 has any teaching about the Negro. While it is true that the African nation makes up most of Canaan's offspring and that a probable etymological meaning of the word Canaan is purple dye, the Negro is not under consideration in any way. As we saw, the principle of division of Chapter 10 is friendship with Israel, not color. And the literary form of Genesis 9:18–27 is an etiology, i.e., a family tree, of the conditions of the Semites (free masters) and Canaanites (slaves) of the author's day; through this etiology, the author teaches both that God is provident and that sin brings a curse while goodness brings a blessing.

It would be nice to sit back and think that the difficulties

of biblical interpretation of Genesis 4–11 are over. Far from
it. Cain's token in Genesis 4:15 is conjectured to be a tatoo
of the ritualistic sacrifice branding the man as a sacred victim.
We do not know perfectly what is meant by the numbers of
the genealogies, especially those pertaining to the age of
generation. The "sons of God" mentioned in Genesis 6:1–6
have always been a knotty problem. Although this passage
is probably a myth teaching mankind's sinfulness, not all
agree on this literary form. But Pius XII said: "God wished
difficulties to be scattered through the Sacred Books inspired
by Him in order that we might be urged to read and scruti-
nize them more intently, and, experiencing in a salutary
manner our own limitations, we might be exercised in due
submission of mind. No wonder if of one or other question
no solution wholly satisfactory will ever be found since sometimes we have to do with matters obscure in themselves and
too remote from our times and our experience; and since
exegesis also, like all other most important sciences, has its
secrets which, impenetrable to our minds, by no efforts what-
soever can be unravelled" (*Divino Afflante Spiritu*, #45).

This is the story of God's acts with men. Man sins and
God is merciful. These eleven chapters are the fitting introduction to the entire Bible. As we mentioned and as we are
about to see in detail, the Bible's theme is God's covenant
with man. He started with mankind, and mankind sinned;
God nevertheless promised ultimate victory to mankind.
Cain, Lamech, and finally again all mankind sinned against
God. God punished them and entered into a second covenant
with all through Noah (Gn 9:8–17). The Tower of Babel
related how mankind, giving in to its proneness to sin,
proudly defied the Omnipotent. God's punishment left us
asking: "Is God's mercy at an end? Will He now no longer
make a covenant with mankind?" The answer is partially
affirmative. By God's covenant with Abraham, mankind was
put aside. God takes to Himself the ancestry of a people
whom He would choose. And yet, despite mankind's repeti-

tious sinning, God would bless all of it in Abraham. Paul understood this blessing as fulfilled in Christ Jesus. "The promises were made to Abraham and to his descendant . . . who is Christ" (Gal 3:16 f.). And you and I and all men were blessed through and in Him.

CHAPTER FOUR

THE COVENANTING WORD

1. The Covenant (Genesis 12–Exodus 24)

"SALVATION comes from the Jews," so our Lord told the Samaritan (cf. Jn 4:22). Why? We do not know any more than that this is simply the way He wanted it. "Does the object molded say to him who molded it, 'Why have you made me thus?'" (Rom 9:20.) How is salvation from the Jews? That we do know. God chose Abraham, Isaac, Jacob, Joseph, and then Moses. The history is the pulsating story of God's dramatic covenant with a people whom He made, saved, wooed, married, lost, won back, and transformed.

In this chapter, we shall see in order the main teachings, literary sources, forms and qualities, history, coarse morality, and some unsolved problems of Genesis 12–Exodus 24. Using ancient traditions, the redactors of these chapters taught God's election of, and covenant with, Israel and His choice and blessing of the Patriarchs. They taught these truths through the animated stories of Abraham, Jacob, Joseph, and Moses.

"Salvation comes from the Jews." How easy it would have been if God had handed out heaven in a test tube or with a vaccinating needle. Instead He chose to work it out through men in historical acts. And, as St. Thomas teaches (cf. *Summa Theologica* I, 22, a 2 ad 2), God, who is supremely perfect, allows some things to be imperfect and yet achieves His end. This is surely verified with salvation. God has allowed finite beings to fail and yet has achieved His end; if you have ever wondered at the tortuous ways of Christian salvation, read attentively the labyrinthian ways of pre-Christian preparation for salvation. God could use the lives of His patriarchs to bring out the promises of land and of innumerable descendants.

How did it all begin? How did God bring about the promise of countless children and a land? For promise He did. In fact, it seems with the hope of that promise He got Abraham to leave his home in Mesopotamia. God looked down on mankind and chose an unknown, insignificant bedouin, Abraham. He chose this seminomad from all the peoples of the world. He promised him again and again that his progeny would be, "As the dust of the earth; if anyone can count the grains of dust, your posterity can also be counted. Arise, walk the length and breadth of the land, for to you I will give it" (Gn 13:16 f.). The biblical account of Abraham is not finished until Christ, it is true. But in the Old Testament it was fulfilled in the possession of Palestine by the nation of Israel. In the meantime, just as now, God worked out the promises.

Promises in his hand, did Abraham go down to the Land of Canaan, take it over, and begin propagating? Not by a long shot. If we had been planning to give the promises, we would probably have arranged things a lot more smoothly and "logically." God disposed all things much more humanly. Abraham wandered from Shechem to Hebron to Egypt and back again. He wandered in the southlands too. Neither was his luck with his offspring any better. Sarah, Abraham's wife, remained barren until he was an old man. Yes, he had a child from a slave, Hagar, but as quickly as that happened so quickly was he told by God that that child, Ishmael, was not the one promised. Only when Abraham was an old man did Sarah give him Isaac, the child of the promise.

Salvation is to come from the Jews and it will be some 2000 years in the coming. In his lifetime Abraham had the blessing and protection of God. He had received promises of a land and offspring, and at his death he had only Isaac as fulfillment. So does God work out salvation. It pleases the

Creator to use human, defective instruments to achieve His ends. Did Abraham's offspring get the promises any more directly? Of Abraham's son, Isaac, little more is known to the biblical compiler than that he had two sons, Jacob and Esau.

Jacob's plight was even worse, naturally speaking, than was that of Abraham, at least as regards the blessing. Practically speaking, he had to steal it by getting Esau to sell it for a mess of pottage and by fraudulently deceiving his father. His lot for getting a wife was little better. Tricked by wily Laban, Jacob wound up with the unloved, ugly Leah while he wanted the children of the promise to come from comely Rachel. After getting Rachel, he had to swindle Laban for his justly due salary. Coming back to the Promised Land, he bribed and hoodwinked Esau, just to avoid getting killed. Rather a common human life for one who had inherited the blessing of God! In fact, we should begin to wonder if God can really give this shrewd sheik, Jacob, the Promised Land and the multitudinous progeny.

Intertwined with all this natural living, were there visions and promises of God? After Jacob had grabbed the firstborn's right to the inheritance, Abraham's God appeared to him and reiterated the blessing (Gn 28:13 f.). Later Jacob wrestled to a draw with "a heavenly being face to face" and received a change in name to Israel, or "strong — striving — with God." If it were not for these incidents and the statement of Genesis 32:10, "Jacob prayed, 'God of my father Abraham and God of my father Isaac, Lord who said to me, "Return to your land and to your kin, and I will deal with you," ' " we might be tempted to forget the true teaching in all of Israel's life. God was working out the promises; He did this with human lives and, for our way of looking at it, a bit too humanly, but then this story of Jacob's life is the divine truth of God's blessing and choice of Israel.

The story of Joseph explains how the people got down into Egypt. It is a story more in keeping, perhaps, with our own notion of how God should work out salvation. Sent into Egypt because of the jealousy of his eleven brothers, Joseph after some ill luck prospered, eventually winning the plenipotentiary power of Pharaoh. He then showed himself to be a forgiving man and brought his own family down to Egypt when a famine covered the earth. All of this was seen as God's providence, disposing all for the good of His chosen race's forefathers; as Joseph told his brothers, "Do not be distressed nor angry with yourselves that you sold me here; for God sent me before you to save life. . . . Not you but God sent me here" (Gn 45:5, 8). The biblical redactor saw things as they truly were: God, having promised Abraham the blessing, used all the vagaries of human situations, temptations, sins, and joys to work out the promise.

God will always be known to the Jews as the God of Abraham, of Isaac, and of Jacob. Very briefly, we have seen the biblical presentation of these men who began salvation's journey. The next 400 years are summarized in one verse in Exodus, "But the Israelites were fruitful and prolific. They became so numerous and strong that the land was filled with them" (Ex 1:7). Thus was accomplished the promise of the progeny as numerous as the sand of the seashore (Gn 22:17). But again the Promised Land will not come by just walking from Egypt to Palestine. The people will be enslaved and saved, will make a pact with God, and then take the Promised Land only by war and bloodshed.

The fulfillment of the first promise of the great progeny seemed almost to undo all chances of the second. When the Egyptian Pharaoh saw how numerous were the Jews, he enslaved them. But God prepared, again through a roundabout path, their savior: Moses. Saved from the bulrushes, trained at the Egyptian court, driven into exile but called to be savior of God's people, this was the preparation of the greatest prophet and lawgiver of Israel. You know the story of the ten plagues and the flight from Egypt. By this flight from Egypt through the Red Sea, God's power was proved to the Israelites. He was the God "Who brought them out of the land of Egypt" (Ex 20:2).

It may be well to dwell a while on this fact of the freedom from slavery. You see, it was the Israelite's "definition" of God. For the Israelite, God was never defined in philosophical terms, for instance, as the one who depends on no one in any way — subsistent being. He was rather viewed in terms of history, of His action on man, and was regarded as the God who brought His oppressed throng out of Egypt. This historical fact remained at the root of all Israel's confessions of faith. God's complete control over nature and men is proved in this historical fact. His redemptive love which saves and uses the weak of the world to accomplish His purpose even among the strong is proved in His delivery from the bondage of Egypt (cf. Appendix I).

As we have seen, the history of Abraham, Jacob, and even Joseph showed little of the omnipotence of God. But surely the God who stole a weak and dispirited mob from the strongest temporal power of the time, such a God could be trusted, come what may.

This is what God told the group before Him, "You have seen for yourselves how I treated the Egyptians and how I bore you up on eagle wings and brought you here to myself. Therefore, if you harken to my voice and keep my covenant, you shall be my special possession, dearer to me than all other people, though all the earth is mine" (Ex 19:4 f.). God had promised Abraham to give him a people and a land. Israel is now free to accept the covenant, God's way of fulfilling His promise. The pact was struck and sealed. By it Israel promised fidelity to God, summarized in the Ten Commandments and especially in a rejection of all alliances since these would imply that God could not protect His people. God, on His part, promised a land and protection no matter how strong the enemy. The rest of the Old Testament tells how God remained faithful to the covenant and how Israel time and again proved faithless.

Salvation comes from the Jews. It comes with all human lack and failing, but it comes. We are now at the main theme of the Bible and have seen its background. God forged a pact with the Israelites. Israel looked back and saw in its forefathers the beginnings of that pact. Just as we, so too Israel stood in awe at this great God, the Creator who would and could use the ill-equipped history of Abraham, Jacob, and Joseph to bring about His promises. That is why He is God. Paul beheld the cross in the same eye of faith, "But we, for our part, preach a crucified Christ — to the Jews certainly a stumbling block and to the Gentiles absurdity, but to those who are called, to the Jews and Greeks alike, Christ, the power of God and the wisdom of God" (1 Cor 1:23 f.). In all of this treatment, therefore, we were not trying to belittle the saintly patriarchs. We were trying to show how great a God is our God, who used these men with all their failings and virtues to achieve so great a salvation.

Their virtues are topics for books in themselves. Abraham was known among the Jews of our Lord's time as the Father of believers (cf. Rom 4). Well did he merit it. From what we have seen of his roving life, we can see how much loyalty toward the God of the promise was demanded of this human. Of course the greatest test of this trust was made concerning the other promise, that of the numberless offspring. His only son, Isaac, born to his old age, Abraham himself was asked by God to slaughter. The pathetic drama is portrayed in consummate pathos in Genesis 22; not one useless word detracts from the author's recital. The author of the Epistle to the Hebrews gives the best commentary on it: "By faith Abraham, when he was put to the test, offered Isaac. He who had received the promise, he to whom it had been said, 'Of Isaac issue will be born to you,' was on the point of sacrificing his only-begotten. He reasoned that God has power to raise men from the dead. Thus Abraham got back his son, who was to serve as a type" (Heb 11:17–19). Which of us Christians has ever been called on for a like test of loyalty? Just passing, let us add that Genesis 18:16–33 gives one of the best examples and teachings on the saving power of a good man and prayer. Abraham prays God to promise not to destroy a city if ten upright men be in it.

Joseph's life was also an act of trust. But perhaps more timely for us is his purity. Chapter 39 tells how he was tempted by a wife of an officer of Pharaoh and refused. For his virtue he was cast into prison.

This section of the Old Testament teaches us God's love for Israel and Israel's forefathers and ultimately for us, since thus did God prepare Christ's coming. The Exodus itself is a proof for us as well as it was for Israel of God's power and disinterested love. A slave had nothing to give God, yet He chose Israel and took this slave from the most powerful of nations!

So much for the theological teaching of this vast section. Its main doctrine is God's love in covenanting with Israel and with Israel's forefathers; its secondary and incidental teaching is the virtues exposed in the lives of the patriarchs. Many other truths (e.g., Moses' fidelity, Passover as a figure of the Crucified, God's presence in the ark and cloud) can be found in this section, but let us now turn to its literary character.

An even stronger argument for the source theory than we mentioned above (pp. 18 f., 27) is immediately evident to all of us who have been reading these chapters of the Bible. As Father Vawter, quoting Father de Vaux, says:

One after another in the Pentateuch we discover doublets, repetitions, and discordances. . . . Twice Abraham risks Sara's honor in making her pass for his sister (12:13 ff. and 20:1 ff.) and the same adventure is told of Isaac and Rebecca in 26:7 ff. The kidnapping of Joseph is told in two ways (by the Madianites, with the intervention of Ruben; by the Ismaelites, with the intervention of Juda: (37:18–36), as is the story of his introduction into Egypt (with Phutipar who entrusts prisoners to him; with an anonymous Egyptian who puts him into prison, 39), and similarly the story of the second journey of Jacob's sons to Egypt (Ruben, then Juda goes surety for Benjamin, 42:37 and 43:9). Moses' father-in-law is sometimes called Raguel (Ex. 2:18, Num. 10:29), and sometimes Jethro (Exodus 3:1), Moses receives the divine vocation twice (Ex. 3 and 6) and the divine name is revealed to him twice, while according to Gen. 4:26 this name already had been known before the flood. There are several different versions of the story of the plagues of Egypt in Ex. 6–12. Twice there is the incident of the waters of Meriba, where the Israelites resisted Yahweh, Ex. 17:7 and Num. 20:13, and countless other analogous cases.

One may say, and it has been said, that it is not unheard of that the same fact should be written twice, that oral accounts delight in repetition, that the primitive mentality is not bound by our logic. But these explanations are insufficient. These parallel accounts are the very constitution of the narrative; they differ in style, vocabulary, and in the way they represent God and His relation to men. They fall into groups by their affinities of language, manner, concepts, their "constants," which determine the parallel lines pursued in the Pentateuch (*A Path Through Genesis,* p. 21 f.).

The redactor uses these sources to best advantage. The stories about Abraham, Jacob, and Joseph are living, breathing, and absorbing. Every detail adds a new picture. Some of these pictures have been capsuled in the descriptive adjectives used when treating the teachings earlier in this chapter. There was the pathos of Genesis 22. Jacob's shrewdness was told in stories, not in abstractions. Genesis 37–50 is the longest continuous story, that of Joseph, which refreshingly teaches God's protection of Joseph and His blessing in preparation for His people.

Chapter 49 of Genesis is probably the literary form called etiology, a family-tree idea. Living centuries after the blessing, the author transposed the places and the history of the twelve tribes into the mouth of Jacob. The reasons for this conclusion and the exact interpretation go a little beyond the space of these pages. Father Vawter (pp. 293–300, *ibid.*) and Father Sutcliffe in the *Catholic Commentary,* p. 203, give a more detailed explanation.

The crossing of the Reed (*sic,* cf. p. 42) Sea (Ex 12:31–15) and the accounts of the plagues (Ex 6–12) are probably very poetical and exaggerated. Something marvelous occurred, but precisely what is lost in the recesses of legend. The truth that an Almighty God led a motley crew out of Egypt is an undeniable statistic as well as a religious fact.

When we have finished with all of this business about the literary forms, you are saying, "Well you have pretty well done away with the history of Genesis and the history of the first twenty-four chapters of Exodus, I hope you know." Far from it. We need to know the literary forms to understand the literal sense of the Bible, which is a religious teaching on God's election and blessing of His people, as we saw. The happenings or statistics of this period have been established by archaeology and the traditions of the Bible are certainly based on statistical cores.

A summary of the happenings of this period of the Bible is in the following paragraph. For much more detail, read the books by Doctors Albright and Wright mentioned in the bibliography.

About 2000 B.C., a great movement from the West occurred in the Fertile Crescent. Among the hordes involved in this movement was a group of hucksters called the 'Apiru, one of whom was Abraham. This movement reached its zenith when one of the groups involved in it, called the Hyksos, subjugated Egypt, ruling from about 1720–1550 B.C. The 'Apiru or Hebrew were friends of the Hyksos, and they were at first favorably received in Egypt after being invited there by Joseph. When the Hyksos fell out of power, the Hebrews were enslaved or made serfs. Moses led perhaps thousands of these Hebrews out of Egypt. Their numbers were swelled by others at Sinai and increased by other Semitic peoples who had lived and remained in Palestine. Precisely when and where the number twelve for the tribes of Israel comes from is unknown. The unity of this conglomeration seems to have been a religious one, around the God who had chosen the Patriarchs and had brought His people out of Egypt and led them, as we shall see in the next chapter, in a conquest of the Holy Land. The stories of the Bible tell this history interestingly and teach God's election of, and covenant with, Israel and the Patriarchs.

After seeing how God has providentially planned the advances in archaeology to keep pace with the advances in literary appreciation of the Bible, we must move on to the question of morality in the section under our consideration. There are some standard objections to the Bible: Abraham's lie to save his own skin (Gn 12:10–20), Jacob's lie to gain the birthright (Gn 27), Lot's daughters being offered to the people of Sodom (Gn 19:8), Lot's daughters sleeping with their own father (Gn 19:30–38), and the revenge of the violation of Dinah (Gn 34).

In all these incidents, biblical inerrancy is not in question. It would be in question only if some mistake could be shown in these stories. Rather the issue is that such immorality is shocking and scandalous in God's book.

Each episode has to be studied in the light of its literary form. If Abraham and Jacob actually did lie, the biblical author tells that the saints of old were real flesh and blood. If their lies are merely legends handed down and not statistics, then the author is showing that God kept His unconditioned promise to Abraham even when the Patriarchs doubted in Him. In this latter explanation, the truth of the lie is not a statistic but a very down-to-earth way of showing God's protection even of the sinner.

Chapter 19:1–29 echoes one of the most treasured of Semitic virtues, that of hospitality. We would see it as an aspect of charity. Our moralists, with this in mind, would probably explain the lesser evil or surrendering Lot's daughters as being preferable to the greater evil of sinning against hospitality. It is however highly questionable if the story ever happened. These verses teach by the abuse of the virtue of hospitality the total depravity of a city which God therefore had to punish. They also teach the protection of God upon the innocent relative of Abraham, Lot.

In the same chapter, the final nine verses are a bitingly ironic answer to Moab and Edom's claim to be descendants of the Patriarchs. Israel answered that they were descendants all right — by incest.

Chapter 34 is difficult. It probably relates through an etiology (cf. p. 39) why it was not necessary to conquer Shechem when the Israelites took Palestine. Suffice it to say, even later Israel, as Genesis 49:5-7 shows, looked on Simeon's and Levi's actions with some disgust.

Onan's sin (38:8–10) was not so much against chastity as against the "levirate law" (cf. Dt 25:5). By it, Onan was obliged to have children for his dead brother, thereby continuing his brother's life.

These stories are not inept for the Bible. The social milieu was that of the compilers' day, not of Christians of the twentieth century. The redactors wrote God's story which is meant for human encouragement and consolation and thus can narrate that even the holy Patriarchs could sin.

Not all the difficulties of Genesis 12–Exodus 24 can be satisfactorily answered as yet. Genesis 49 has many difficult verses. The Red Sea of Exodus should be translated the Reed Sea (cf. CCD translation, footnote to Ex 10:19). The Reed Sea is most likely a shallow marsh at the northern summit of the Red Sea. The number of people who left Egypt is still disputed. Their precise journey is not certain, as is the cause of their union. If not racial or ethnic, was it purely religious? The etymology of the name of Israel's God, "Yahweh," remains disputed (cf. Appendix I). Time and God's wisdom must be waited upon to give us all the understanding that we need. But if ever that comes, maybe men will forget to read the Bible and to learn its timeless truths of God's love for the only too human humankind.

The Bible contains timeless truths about God. It tells the man of faith about the world's greatest Lover. After creating the world and being rejected by it, He still chose not to punish it by completely destroying it. He befriended one of its peoples so as to bless all the world. The history of this God's actions with faithless man makes absorbing, pulsating drama. It should — even that which concerns Abraham, Isaac, Jacob, the people of Israel covenanting with God. All of this should absorb us; it is the initiation of the drama of our own salvation. You see, we as believers say:

> My father was a wandering Aramean who went down to Egypt with a small household and lived there as an alien. But there he became a nation great, strong, and numerous. When the Egyptians maltreated and oppressed us, imposing hard labor upon us, we cried to the Lord, the God of our fathers, and He heard our cry and saw our affliction, our toil and our oppression. He did bring us out of Egypt with his strong hand and outstretched arm, with terrifying power, with signs and wonders; and bringing us into this country, he gave us this land flowing with milk and honey (Dt 26:5-9).

2. God's Fidelity to the Covenant (Exodus 15–2 Kings)

> Hearken my people to my teaching; Incline your ears to the words of my mouth. . . . I will utter mysteries from of old. . . . The glorious deeds of the Lord and His strength, And the wonders that He wrought (Ps 77:1, 2, 4).

The pact is struck and agreed upon. The symbolic ceremony of the sprinkling of the blood has united God and Israel into one family (Ex 24:3-8). The chief reciprocal virtue is fidelity. The outcome of the covenant is recorded history. In this and the following sections we shall treat the same biblical books. Each section presents in order the main teachings, the literary qualities, and the history of these books. This section adds a note on the morality of the books under consideration; it stresses God's fidelity as its chief teaching. The following section emphasizes Israel's infidelity.

The infinite Creator stepped into history to arrange it, usually using human or natural agents, to the benefit of His people. He gave them a land, maintained them in it, protected them against overpowering enemies, and would eventually have given them the Messiah, but they rejected Him, not once but countless times.

God had chosen to manifest His love in and to the Israelitic people. He had brought them out of Egypt and made this conglomeration into a united people. As they wandered toward the Promised Land in the Sinai Desert, He had given them sweetened waters (Ex 15:22–27), quail, and the famous manna (Ex 16). He had commanded Moses to strike the rock so as to give the people water (Ex 17:1–7), and won the first of many battles (Ex 17:8–16). Yes, these people had indeed experienced God's power, even before the covenant.

His blessings continued after the covenant. When the people complained about the monotony of the manna, He gave them some more quail (Nm 11:1–9, 18–23, 31–34) which turned out to be a medicinal punishment. Although some of these events were miraculous, at least in the way and time that they were produced, God used human agents to work out His promises. Moses was the leader from Egypt and through the stormy times of the wilderness even to the very mountain overlooking the Promised Land.

Then it was that Israel for the first time as a group looked over into the land promised to Abraham and to them at Sinai. At most a land of about 10,000 square miles of uneven arability, it was to a desert wanderer a land of "milk and honey." Although the Promised Land was not paradise, to one who had seen nothing for years except the desert, the Promised Land with its varieties of hills and plains, mountains and seacoasts was the place of rest. This word "rest" has theological significance both in Deuteronomy and Joshua for the place of quiescence and joy in this life. And since the people knew no other life than this life (cf. p. 87), the Promised Land with its verdure, its crops, vineyards, and rainfall came closer to heaven than anything a desert dweller can think of.

This land was already fairly well inhabited. God, however,

would give it to Israel, "Hear, O Israel! You are now about
to cross the Jordan to enter in and dispossess nations greater
and stronger than yourselves, having large cities fortified to
the sky" (Dt 9:1). Indeed, God's power worked great deeds,
for Joshua controlled the central hill country when he captured Jericho and Ai and brought the Gibeonites into the
Sinaitic Alliance (Jos 6–9). He then swung to the south and,
avoiding Jerusalem, took the territory which the tribe of
Judah would later occupy (Jos 10). To the north he also
took some territory, although only Hazor of the fortified cities
fell. The teaching of the Book of Joshua is that "one man
with God can rout a thousand."

The Promised Land had been taken, or had it? In the Book
of Judges, we read that a "mopping-up" campaign was still
going on. "Since the Lord was with Judah he gained poses-
sion of the mountain region. Yet he could not dislodge those
who lived on the plain, because they had iron chariots (Jgs
1:19).

God's way is to use human ways. Joshua had conquered
with the strength of the Lord of Hosts, but more had to be
done. To remove the pockets of pagans that were still resist-
ing, God raised up judges, men for the occasion, sent to
remove a persecutor. God's spirit, a divine propulsion for
some particular task, fell upon the judges. The warrior
Othniel (Jgs 3:8–11), the left-handed dagger-wielder Ehud
(Jgs 3:12–36), Shamgar who killed 600 Philistines (Jgs
3:31) are a few in the list of God's champions. Some are
even more famous: Samson (Jgs 13–16), Gideon and his
three hundred (Jgs 6–8). The judges were taken from every
walk of life. Japthe (Chap. 11) was even a bandit chief
who immolated his daughter as a vowed victim. As was said,
the Lord's spirit moved men to be heroes to do God's work
when repentance brought Israel back to the covenant. Chapter 2 of Judges summarizes the concrete theology of this book
(2:13–19). The theological point of interest for us at present is God's love of His repentant people, shown in men

who, for a short time, were the military leaders of the people.

That "for a short time" finally stuck in the people's craw. The last judge, Samuel, entreated the Lord to give the people a king. And God's goodness gave them their request. He was God's anointed, this king, one chosen by God and acting in God's place — at least this was God's plan for this change in the covenant relation. The first king was of royal size and stood a head over any other Israelite (1 Sm 10:23). Saul was his name. The Lord's spirit stayed with him leading him through victories over the eastern boundary plunderers: Moabite, Ammonite (1 Sm 14:47); and, on the west, the Philistines (1 Sm 14:1–16). Disobedience and pride (1 Sm 13:5–18; 15) gained for him God's rejection and David's choice.

With the Lord's victories through David (1 Sm 16–2 Kgs 1), Israel for the first and last time controlled the entire Promised Land. It has been slow in coming, but faith teaches us that God had shown Himself loyal to His part of the bargain. He had been constantly protecting them, and — give reasons though we will that this puny mob could have remained a people as long as it did — we cannot be satisfied by an answer of the weakness of the other great powers. By reason of its geographical position Palestine was the cross-roads of the ancient world, the only bridge of arable land between Babylon and Egypt. Both of these great powers and others coveted it, but God defended it as long as the people would rely on Him alone.

God proved in the time of Joshua, the Judges, and David that he could and wanted to give and maintain the land for the people. He proved it again about 300 years later (700 B.C.) when He drove the army of Sennacherib, the Assyrian conqueror, from the very gates of Jerusalem. The scene described in 2 Kings 18:17–19:34 agrees substantially with Sennacherib's own chronicle. It relates that Sennacherib had Hezekiah caged up in Jerusalem like a bird, but Sennacherib never says that the Lord freed His faithful Hezekiah. The truth is implied however even by Sennacherib since he never mentions the capture of Jerusalem.

The God of Abraham and Jacob, the God of the Covenant of Sinai had been faithful to His pact, to His agreement with the people of Israel. He had given the people the land and protected them. Despite His fidelity the people rarely kept their part of the agreement; they did not show loyalty to God. Treason is a harsh word, but treason it was for them not to be loyal to the God who brought them out of Egypt. The history of this faithless people will be discussed in the next section.

The main teaching we have been developing is God's fidelity in the covenant. We have omitted many others. The main theology of the first two Books of Samuel is that the ideal king, David, received a promise of an everlasting dynasty from God. Within these books, Chapters 4 to 6 of 1 Samuel teach God's omnipotence and Israel's sin. 1 Samuel 9–31 teaches that God's anointed, Saul, could sin and lose God's election. Indeed, these books are pregnant with meaning. A few examples of the virtues of the heroes of the time follow. Remember, too, these men lived with no thought of a reward after death (cf. p. 87).

Moses, of course, is the paragon for the community led by him from Egypt and established in Palestine. Surely he sinned. But his entire life is, for all Christians and Jews, an example of stalwart dedication to a thankless task. For a model of effective prayer the victory gained by his intercession will be a consolation to anyone, "As long as Moses kept his hands raised up, Israel had the better of the fight, but when he let his hands rest, Amalec had the better of the fight" (Ex 17:11).

The charming narrative of Ruth's filial piety, her spirit of self-sacrifice, and her moral integrity can inspire any disconsolate wife and mother. This is the story of the Book of Ruth, a narrative that gives us insight into the times of Israel's youth.

Eli's sons will always be a reminder to priests of their sins
(1 Sm 2:12–4:22). Saul preferred sacrifice to obedience
(1 Sm 15:22) and lost an everlasting kingdom for his choice
(1 Sm 13:13).

But, of all the figures of this historical period, David is
perhaps the most alluring. Human in his love of man (his
love of Jonathan in 1 Samuel) and woman (i.e., Bathsheba,
2 Sm 11) and his own child (2 Sm 18), he proved himself
so human as deserving divine mercy in his repentance (2
Sm 12).

The above few pages give a sampling of the vast amount
of material found in more than seven books of the Bible. It
is hoped that they will encourage you to read the Bible. The
theological significance of God's covenant and of the examples of virtue are clear enough in the Bible; they are never
preached at us but are lived. Let us now briefly see some
of the literary qualities of this section.

Many of the stories in it are exciting: Joshua at Jericho
(Jos 6); Jonathan's single-handed victory over the Philistines
(1 Sm 14); the biblical mixture of Robin Hood and Richard
the Lionhearted, David (1 Sm 16–1 Kgs 2). Yes, few hearts
would not be stirred by Samson (Jgs 13–16). The skill of
the author must be effective; just think of the many movies
that have been made around these narratives: Ruth, Samson
and Delilah, the Ten Commandments. . . .

Joshua's battle of Jericho has probably a twofold source,
as it is found in the Bible. One describes a silent march for
seven days until a cry breaks the silence; the other describes
a procession with priests and sacred trumpets and the Ark.

Worse the luck for Galileo Galilei that he did not live
after the era of literary criticism. At all events, the famous
incident of the sun's stopping in Joshua 10 can, on scientific
literary principles, be shown to be a double narrative. Verses
8 to 10 probably tell the victory as a somewhat embellished
statistic. Verses 12 to 15 are a short epic describing the
same event through the eyes and with the license of a poet.

Remember in all of this — epic poem or historical account — the doctrine is the same: God caused the victory for His coveted and covenanted people. Thus the Book of Judges in general can be shown to be an artificial arrangement of stories which are based on four steps: fault, chastisement, repentance, and liberation. Deborah's canticle in Chapter 5, which is so ancient that it may be dated about 1125 B.C., is an excellent example of the early Hebrew poetical style. The poet has a way with words, easier to remember the truth after his balancing hand finished with it.

The Bible's fable (Jgs 9:8–15) appears in this story. Riddles in the legendary Samson's mouth (Jgs 14:10–18) become the death of thirty men from the Philistine city of Ashkelon. One of our favorite Old Testament passages is David's eulogy of his friend, Jonathan: "As the mother loveth her only son, so did I love thee, Jonathan" (2 Sm 1:20–27).

The stories of heroes, riddles, poems, eulogies — who could not find some fascinating reading in these chapters? Yet, although the final edition of most of these books was hundreds of years after the events, science has come to prove that they are in the main historically accurate. The findings of archaeology dovetail with the account of the cities captured, the iron age, the dwellings of the Egyptian Pharaohs as told in the Bible's Exodus and the capture of the Holy Land.

One would have to read the books on archaeology mentioned in the bibliography to appreciate the minute confirmation of many of the biblical stories. The history of these times can be summarized as follows: About 1300 B.C. Moses led some of the Hebrews out of Egypt. After wandering through the desert, about 1250 B.C., Joshua led the people into Palestine. Groups of Hebrews already living in Palestine (descendants of Abraham who had not gone into Egypt) joined them and, under Joshua's leadership, a substantial control of the hill country of Palestine fell to the Hebrews. Charismatic leaders called judges finished the operation of controlling most of Palestine and warded off foreign invaders during the 1100's. The last judge, Samuel, introduced unwillingly (cf. p. 46) the king, Saul, who ruled about 1020–1004 B.C. David (1004–965 B.C.) conquered all of Palestine. After Solomon's absolute potentate (965–926 B.C.), the land was divided into two kingdoms. The northern kingdom ruled by many dynasties fell to the Assyrians in 721 B.C. The southern kingdom under the Davidic king lasted until the Babylonian conquest in 587 B.C.

In the process of recounting these seven hundred years of history, the biblical writers assembled some rather unseemly stories. At least we Christians tend to see some coarseness in their moral code. God's command to totally destroy nations appears in full bloom (1 Sm 15:2 f., etc.). This destruction is the famous *kerem* or ban or consecrated massacre, practiced by the people of those days. Is the Bible teaching that God commanded the *kerem?* While it is true that the Semite makes no distinction between permissive and imperative causality, we do not think that this principle should be invoked here — at least in any way as an apology for the biblical teaching.

Some explain these incidents as primitive morality. There is a certain truth in this. Surely the revelation of "turning the other cheek" had not yet been given. But how can we say this is primitive when we have the massacres in Dachau, in Hungary, and in Hiroshima in these advanced days of revelation?

We prefer to explain the command of God as His judgment on a people who had refused to bend to His helping grace. Since the pagan people refused to be converted and live with the people of God's choice, they had to be killed by God's instrument, Israel. This sentence is no worse than having an executioner deal out the judge's death penalty. It is no worse than the tornado's killing hundreds of people. God permits or causes all of this. The only difference is that the Bible realistically attributes the event to God, who is, after all, its cause.

The Bible is never mealymouthed. The God of the Bible is a living, loving God, who really entered human history. The Bible recounts life as it happened, with all its beauty and some of its ugliness. If God judged that a people deserved annihilation and decreed that the Israelites be His avenging annihilator, the Bible described that too. Only a Jansenistic better-than-God Christian would cluck his tongue at God's inspired truth and reality.

David's sin with Bathsheba (2 Sm 11) has already been mentioned. It is as known as any incident of the Old Testament. David's sin in causing Uriah, her husband, to die with a number of other soldiers is much more grievous. May his repentance and forgiveness be equally well known. None of these should be a cause of shock for one believing in the power of the all-merciful God. God's mercy, yes! We did not even mention it in all the above. And yet it is as important and evident a teaching as His affective love in the wonders of nature and victorious battles. The author of the 135th Psalm grasps the idea in his contemplation of God's acts in history:

> Give thanks to the Lord, for He is good, for his mercy endures forever; who alone does great wonders, for his mercy endures forever; who made the heavens in wisdom, for his mercy endures forever; who smote the Egyptians in their first-born, for his mercy endures forever; who smote great kings, for his mercy endures forever; and made their land a heritage, for his mercy endures forever; who remembered us in our abjection, for his mercy endures forever; give thanks to the God of heaven, for his mercy endures forever.

3. Jewish Infidelity (Exodus 24–2 Kings)

"For his mercy endures forever." We just finished depicting God's love. Its depth is meaningful only when it is viewed against the people's sins. There were the sins of the golden calf, the murmuring about the manna, the rebellion at the very border of the Promised Land. There was the disloyalty of demanding a king to rule, and turning to foreign nations for protection. The Israelites as a society were in agreement with the Lord; they had accepted the Ten Commandments and their chief virtue was to have been loyalty to the God who had rescued them. Loyalty found its expression especially in not having any foreign alliances. The people sinned and God was merciful. It is easy enough for us to say, "How could they have!" But, understood in the historical period of their times, their sin is more one of weakness than contempt.

In the preceding section we reviewed the teachings of these biblical books from the aspect of God's gifts; let us now glance over the same books — which cover some 700 years — from the people's viewpoint. By grasping the historical circumstances surrounding the events described, we can at least see why the Israelites were unfaithful to God; their sin becomes intelligible if, for all that, not excusable.

The covenant had barely been struck when the people sinned. They wanted to have an image of the Lord. After all, other peoples had images of their gods. Why should not the Israelites have a golden calf to remind them of their God? Exodus 20:3 said in part: "You shall not crave idols for yourselves." No sooner made than broken was this covenant. Through Moses' intercession (Ex 32:11–13), the Lord did not immediately rescind His agreement, "They made a calf in Horeb and adored a molten image" (Ps 105:19), "for His mercy endures forever."

Sin though it was, was it not understandable how the Israelites, having seen figurines of the Egyptians, would not wish to imitate them? After the golden calf, other sins followed. They murmured at the monotonous diet of manna. "We remember the fish we used to eat without cost in Egypt, and the cucumbers, the melons, the leeks, the onions, and the garlic. But now we are famished; we see nothing before us but this manna" (Nm 11:4–9). The Egyptians' fleshpots were not extremely appetizing, but the miraculous manna was tiresome. Small gratitude for a meal given without cost, and which was theirs for the gathering. The Lord satisfied them, giving them quail which made them sick and die. His medicinal punishment did not help their memories for long, however.

As they came to the Holy Land itself, their scouts reported that the land was rich and desirable, yes. But its inhabitants were fierce and strong (Nm 13:33): "Veritable giants; we felt like mere grasshoppers." A trek through that barren Sinai Desert would make any man's heart quiver. The thought of a rabble, as Israel was at the time, having to go up against giants would make the greatest believer in God hesitate. Throughout the past years, they had wandered from water hole to water hole. They had had to avoid rebellious nomadic tribes. And now this! They were expected to war against this tribe of giants. Humanly speaking, their diffidence was understandable. Remember though, the prime virtue of the covenant was loyalty, a fidelity which was to be proved in the most trying of circumstances. Israel refused to go up to battle, and the Lord, although not abrogating the covenant, sentenced the entire group to wander throughout the lifetime of a generation through this bleak desert (Nm 14). The prophet Amos (5:25 f.) and the Acts of the Apostles (7:42 f.) imply that there was wholesale apostasy and a turning to worship the false god, Moloch, during these forty years. The Lord, nevertheless, ultimately did bring His people to the Promised Land and through the hands of Josuah, conquered it for His people.

Once in the Promised Land, however, the people did not always obey God. "An angel of the Lord went up from Gilgal to Bochim and said, 'It was I who brought you up from Egypt and led you into the land which I promised on oath to your fathers. I said that I would never break my covenant with you but that you were not to make a pact with the inhabitants of this land, and you were to pull down their altars. Yet you have not obeyed me'" (Jgs 2:1 f.). The Israelites' sin during the time of the Judges is not always particularized. At the time of Othniel, idolatry was the sin, "Because the Israelites had offended the Lord by forgetting

the Lord their God, and serving the Baals and Asheras" (Jgs
3:7). They did sin. Small wonder! They were living separated
from one another, broken roughly into twelve tribes. Between
the tribes were the former inhabitants and their gods. What
was more natural than to join forces with these people? A
foreign alliance brought the inevitable worship of false gods.
Both allegiance and worship of false gods, though natural
enough, remained sins against the covenant alliance with the
Lord, their unique God.

Perhaps Israel reasoned that instead of many and occa-
sional chiefs, if only it had one permanent leader, then it
would and could be loyal to the Lord. The Philistines were
a menace not to one or another tribe but to the very existence
of all the people. Let the Israelites have a king like the other
nations then. It is the only sensible thing to do. Natural
enough, so to reason! It was a breaking of the covenant however. Chapter 8 of 1 Samuel explains the insidious sin. The
covenant said that the Lord was to rule, and no earthly king.
The people would begin to rely on an earthly king, not God.
By asking for a king, then, they were being disloyal to the
Omnipotent. The Bible teaches, "The Lord said to Samuel,
'. . . They [the people] have not rejected thee, but me, that
I should not reign over them' " (1 Sm 8:7). The people no
longer trusted the Lord in the original organization of the
covenant.

Kings David and Solomon, on the whole, were loyal, at
least publicly, and the covenant was a public pact. After
Solomon's death, the kingdom was divided: the South (Judah) with two tribes and the North (Israel) with ten. The
moral climate in Judah was not as bad as that in Israel.
Judah sinned by worshiping the Lord illicitly and by a certain
amount of open idolatry. Israel's sin was more flagrant; it is
called the "sin of Jeroboam," a golden calf or bull which
was the throne of the Lord. King Jeroboam, fearing that
his people would go to worship at the Temple of Jerusalem,
erected sanctuaries in Dan and Bethel where his people could

worship. "Let their pilgrimages terminate in the Northern Kingdom," he reasoned, "otherwise I shall soon lose my people." These illicit shrines remained through the 300-year history of the Northern Kingdom, an illicit cult and an occasion of idolatry.

In addition to sinful worship, both Judah and Israel entered into agreements with foreign powers. Sometimes Syria, sometimes Assyria, sometimes Egypt, sometimes Babylon. No matter who the ally might be, a public agreement with a foreign power showed a lack of confidence in God's strength, and thus was a sin against Him. But what should these two dwarfs of nations do? What was more natural than to rely on the giants to the north and the south? But their pact with the Lord was supernatural, just as He and His power are.

After the sins of the golden calf, murmuring, demand of a king, the faithless pacts, and idolatrous worshiping, after some 700 years of sinning, the covenant was ended in 587 B.C. with the Exile. We shall turn to the Exile later (cf. p. 80).

> Hearken my people to my teaching. The glorious deeds of the Lord and His strength. So that the generation to come might know . . . and not forget the deeds of God. . . . And not be like their fathers, a generation wayward and rebellious, a generation that kept not its heart steadfast nor its spirit faithful toward God (Ps. 77:1, 4, 7, 8).

God's demand for complete loyalty and the faithlessness of the people are the major points brought out in these books of the Old Testament. The people's lack of faith and trust contrasts sadly with the acts of loving mercy which God, as seen in the previous section, worked on their behalf. There are other secondary teachings. One of these is God's chastisement for sin. Many examples may be found. Some have been mentioned: the forty years' wandering in the desert resulting from fear to attack immediately (Nm 14); the quail that caused death (Nm 11); the overrunning of the land during the period of the Judges because of the people's disobedience (cf. Jgs.).

Among the most famous examples of individual sinners are Ahab, a king of Israel, and his wife Jezebel. Jezebel tried to uproot the worship of the Lord altogether. She is most remembered for her murdering theft of the vineyard of Naboth, which was coveted by her childishly churlish husband (1 Kgs 21). That husband, Ahab, died and dogs licked his blood (1 Kgs 22:29–40). Jezebel's fate was little better: bedecked as a vamp, she was cast down from an upper floor (2 Kgs 9:26–37), "And when they went to bury her they found nothing but the skull, and the feet and the extremities of her hands" (2 Kgs 9:35).

The prophets Elijah and Elisha appeared during this period. Their lives showed the victorious Lord at work, performing miracle after miracle (1 Kgs 17–2 Kgs 13). Every type of miracle from raising the dead to making rain can be listed among their accomplishments. So mighty is the Lord, the God of Israel.

Though the prayer of Elijah was great in ending the three years of drought (1 Kgs 18:41–45), it had been bettered by the frequent examples of Moses' intercession for his sinful people. One example is Numbers 14:10–25. Moses convinced the Lord that He owed it to Himself not to exterminate this ungrateful mob.

The final example for us is the gift of wisdom given to Solomon. He spoke many parables and proverbs. His wisdom even traveled as far as the Queen of Sheba (1 Kgs 10). The example given by the compiler of the Book of Kings is known to all of you: the division of the baby of the harlot (1 Kgs 3:16–28).

This ends our treatment of the disloyalty of Israel toward God and of a few examples of famous sinless and sinful people. We summarized the archaeological confirmations of the substantial historicity of the biblical account on page 49. An interesting note which comes from about 1220 B.C. is the oldest mention of Israel in contemporary inscriptions. Most of the text is devoted to a triumphal poem celebrating the Pharaoh's victory over the Libyans. The inscription says, "Israel has been laid waste, it has no offspring."

The literary beauty of this huge section of the Bible has also been noted on page 42. Let us in passing allude to the Canticle of Anna (1 Sm 2:1–10), upon which Mary's *Magnificat* may depend. Too, the Canticle of Moses can now be better appreciated since its theology of fidelity and infidelity fits into a better historical background. God is truly "The Rock, how faultless are his deeds. A faithful God, without deceit. Yet, basely has he been treated by his degenerate children" (Dt 32:1–43). The golden calf incident may well be a later interpretation of some sin made explicit from the famous sin of Jeroboam.

In this and the preceding sections we have followed the biblical presentation of theology — God in His covenant. A more systematized exposition of the main teachings of these books will help summarize these two chapters. Exodus teaches that the Lord God was powerful enough to lead Israel from Egypt and loving enough to strike a covenant.

Deuteronomy uses the covenant form to orate that God's revealed will is the Law. The Book of Josuah exemplifies that "one man can, with God's power, rout a thousand." Judges shows God's saving love for His repentant people.

The two Books of Samuel have as one of their principal lessons the eternal dynasty promised to David, the ideal king. The two Books of Kings explain that not God, but the kings' sins, were the cause of the fall of Palestine.

Leviticus details God's will for sacrifices, ordinations, legal cleanness, and holiness. These laws separated Israel totally from its pagan neighbors and dedicated the nation to God. Numbers enumerates God's people. It gives examples of Israel's waywardness from God in its journey to the Promised Land. God's protection for His own and punishment for evil are exemplified.

Don't you agree that the Bible teaches the drama of God's fidelity and Israel's treason more interestingly than a schematic theology does?

May Deuteronomy's compiler help us to the understanding that was his when he penned the theology of the covenant:

> How could one man rout a thousand, or two men put ten thousand to flight, unless it was because their Rock sold them and the Lord delivered them up? Indeed their "rock" is not like our Rock, and our foes are under condemnation (Dt 32:30 f.).

We can understand a bedouin from the desert whose eyes had seen the breathtaking sight of Jebel Musa (Moses' Mount) and who could use this as a symbol of matchless, immovable strength. Yes, the Lord was his rock, faithful — no matter what:

> Learn then that I, I alone am God and there is no god besides me. It is I who bring life and death, I who inflict wounds and heal them, and from my hand there is no rescue (Dt 32:39).

CHAPTER FIVE

THE PROPHETIC WORD

How true it is, "from my hand there is no rescue." Not that God had not tried to keep the people from falling into His punishing hand. He had sent prophets to incite His people to heed the obligations that they had freely accepted in the covenant. Fidelity to God was their prime duty, as we have seen. The Ten Commandments summarized their other obligations. To the spirit of these ten, the prophets called the people.

Amos inveighed against social injustices. Isaiah denounced bribery and oppression of the weak. Jeremiah demanded obedience. Ezekiel condemned hypocrisy. And so on, the three major (Isaiah, Jeremiah, and Ezekiel) and twelve minor (Hosea, Joel, Amos, Obadiah, Jonah, Micah, Nahum, Habakkuk, Zephaniah, Haggai, Zechariah, and Malachi) prophets berated Israel's sins.

These prophets were God's spokesmen. At times, they foretold the future but their primary task was to speak on God's behalf. God had chosen them to encourage and admonish, to console and chide His people. They were colorful figures. Singularly lonely, often imitated, they were more often held up to raillery and derision.

In the following paragraphs we give their teachings, something about their personality when known, the literary qualities of their writings, and a cursory sketch of their times and place.

AMOS

Jeroboam II (c. 786–746 B.C.) reigned in the Northern Kingdom of Israel. The North had just won a great victory (760–750). For the first time in years, Damascus, the capital

of Syria, itself had fallen under the yoke of Israel. The
shepherd (7:10–17) Amos, in an unmitigated invective,
condemned Israel for social injustices. The freed slave, Israel,
was itself now enchaining its own poor (2:6–8). Piously
prattling their sacrifices to God (5:21–27), the people oppressed the poor, the orphans, and the widows. Amos
rhapsodized in an elaborate style of denunciations and paren-
thetic interruptions. Yes, Amos threatened, the Day of the
Lord, a time of retribution, will come to blind Israel. It has
broken God's covenant by its social sins (5:18; 9:1–4).

HOSEA

Speaking about 740–730, Hosea is talking to an Israel
that has begun to feel the pressure of the mammoth Assyria.
It is an Israel whose internal political situation has weakened
almost to chaos. His writing is one of the most symbolic of
the Bible. His life is the most symbolic.

With a boldness that surprises and a passion that astounds,
the tender and violent soul of Hosea has expressed for the
first time the relations of God and Israel in terms of marriage.
All his message has for its fundamental theme is the love of
God misunderstood by His wife, Israel. Israel has become a
harlot.

Hosea takes to task especially the rulers. Kings, by entering
foreign alliances, have degraded the chosen people. Priests,
ignorant and rapacious, lead to disaster.

Hosea is the prophet of love. The passionate burning love
of God for His wayward people is expressed in Chapters 1–3
and 11–14. Hosea could express such an emotion, for he
had been ordered by God to marry a woman who, he knew,
would play the prostitute. He waited for her return. So too,
God waits for the return of Israel.

Two tensions are found in Hosea. They may be summarized, "How can a lover chastise?" The solution found by
Hosea's God: a medicinal punishment to make the beloved
an object of even greater love (cf. below, Chapter Eight)."

ISAIAH

Based on the principle that prophecy *may* have been written before what it predicts, but that it must have been composed after what it presupposes, almost all independent scholars and many Catholic scholars divide the biblical Book of Isaiah into three parts. Chapters 1–39 constitute the first part and the section that we will be considering now. Chapters 40–55, sometimes called Second Isaiah, are generally attributed to an anonymous poet who prophesied about 540 B.C. during the exile of the people in Babylon. Chapters 56–66 contain oracles from a later period and were composed by disciples who inherited the spirit and continued the work of the great prophet. We will see Second Isaiah and Third Isaiah later.

Isaiah's preaching spans half a century. Shortly after the time of Hosea about 740 B.C., he began. He died in unknown circumstances about 687 B.C. By any measure, Isaiah is a poetical genius. Looking on the entire matter, one author has called it a rhapsody set to words. Isaiah compresses the most picturesque figures into the most succinct phrases. Vivid, impressionistic, energetic, precise — his every word delineates nature, humans, even the majesty of the Unutterable.

Some of the most well known of Old Testament passages come from Isaiah. Chapter 6 is the scene of the heavenly court chanting "Holy, holy, holy is the Lord of hosts!" The unworthy Isaiah, cleansed by God, becomes eager to accept the frustrating task of preaching to a people who will refuse him. Chapter 5:1–7 describes the vineyard of the Lord, an allegory on the refusal of Israel to accept God and its need for punishment.

Isaiah speaks of the Messiah especially in Chapters 7–9 and 11. These chapters present thorny problems for exegetes. A book of this type allows us to present only the most recent conclusions about the literal sense of Isaiah's teaching. The chapters involve roughly thirty-five years of history (c. 734–

700 B.C.). In 7:14, Isaiah's literal sense is that Emmanuel
(King Hezekiah — ?) is the hope of God's promised Davidic
royal Messiah (cf. teaching of the Books of Samuel, p. 57
above). Chapter 9:5 f. teaches that the North (Israel) can
rely on God to raise up the Davidic promised king whose
rule will be the Lord's in its wisdom, strength, and endurance.
His kingdom will reign by the covenant virtues of holiness
and piety. Isaiah leaves open the question whether this confidence will find ultimate rest in King Hezekia. In 11:1–9,
Isaiah teaches that the Messiah will come in some future time.
He will be holy. His efficient, resolute wisdom will be the
Lord's own. His era will bring unheard-of peace. You and I,
in the fullness of Christian revelation, know that Emmanuel
is Jesus of Nazareth and His kingdom of peace is the Mystical
Body. God taught this in Isaiah in a fuller sense (cf. p. 6 f.).

Four paradoxes worthy of long meditation summarize
Isaiah's message: (1) God's holiness and Israel's sinfulness;
(2) Israel's stubbornness and God's redemption; (3) Zion
(Jerusalem) destroyed and Zion saved; (4) Israel in igno-
miny and Israel in glory. Somehow through the sinfulness
of Israel and the punishment of God, a remnant would escape
from Zion to show God's saving power!

MICAH

Micah gives essentially the same teaching as Isaiah and
Amos: the sin of the people is social injustice. His preaching
probably dates between 725 and 697 B.C. and was hurled
against the Southern Kingodm of Judah. He is preoccupied
chiefly with the lot of the poor, rural classes, exploited by
the rich landowners of Judah. In style and content, his prophecies resemble those of Amos in their vehement denunciation
of abuses and threats of chastisement. The entire book may
be divided into two general and not exclusive parallel statements: the certainty of judgment (1:2–16; 6:1 f); accusa-
tions of injustice and oppressions (2:1–3:12; 6:3–7:10 —
this latter section is a dramatic presentation of the Lord's

arraigning His people before the court of the everlasting hills); and restoration through destruction (Chapters 4 and 5 and 7:11–20).

NAHUM

The stirring prophecy of Nahum is dated about 612 B.C. It was written on the eve of the fall of Nineveh, the capital of the Nazilike kingdom of Assyria. Its prophecy is unique in the Old Testament. It is filled with exultant joy at God, revenger of evil! It expresses deep faith in God's omnipotent power. The Lord is sovereign of the world! Nahum's concept of history as playing out the providence of God is a profound theological truth. Isaiah saw God even in Israel's stubbornness. Jeremiah perceived Him in the chastisement of His beloved people. Nahum confesses Him justly avenging the wrongs of Assyria.

ZEPHANIAH

During the 620's, the kingdom of Judah under the fine king Josiah had been busily asserting its independence and reestablishing its control over the whole of western Palestine. At this time Zephaniah and Jeremiah began their prophetic careers. Zephaniah's message may be summarized in the announcement of the Day of the Lord, an impending catastrophic judgment which awaits all the Gentiles as well as Judah. Judah is condemned for its faults — religious and moral — which are inspired by a sense of pride and revolt (3:1–11). Zephaniah has profound insights into the meaning of sin, for he sees it as a personal attack on the living God.

He wishes Judah to view the Gentiles' punishment as a forewarning (3:7). The punishment ought to bring the people to obedience and humility (2:3). Salvation is promised to the humble and modest remnant (3:12 f.).

Zephaniah was correct in his fears. Assyria was soon replaced by another power. About 605 B.C., the Babylonians conquered Egypt and Palestine.

HABAKKUK

This prophet meditated on the power of evil. Babylonia was devastating the Holy Land at that time (c. 590 B.C.). How can God permit this? His answer came in clear terms: trust in God, loyalty to Him even in the face of the most trying obstacles. "The just man, because of his faith, shall live" (2:4). Habakkuk's is a timeless though self-effacing teaching. Is the test of the man of God the sinfulness of his fellows? Let him show his fidelity. Is his understanding unable to grasp the victory of sinful nations? Let him be loyal. Does he ask why the more sinful harm the better? Let him trust in God's power, wisdom, and love one day to punish. Has he lost all natural security? Let him know he will live if he remains steadfastly adhering to the Lord's will! Faith, hope, charity — come what may!

JEREMIAH

Jeremiah is the most personable of the Old Testament prophets. This results from two causes. First, we know more about his life than any other personality of the Bible except David and Jesus. Second, we humans appreciate his timidity, his complaints, and his suffering.

Jeremiah's career extended from 626 B.C. to about 585 B.C. His writing contains statistics, (auto)biography, and rhapsodic elements. All his figures are striking and some are memorable (9:20 f.; 31:15 f.). He was vibrantly sensitive to nature's relation to God.

Three divisions help us understand his message. The first twenty-five chapters group diverse sayings. Chapters 26–45 are his biography. Chapters 46–51 prophesy the destruction of the Gentiles, i.e., the pagan nations surrounding and threatening the Israelites.

Shy and sensitive by nature, Jeremiah's stammering, "Ah, ah, ah," was strengthened in his call to God's ministry to a "for I am with you to deliver you, says the Lord" (1:1–19).

Not that he did not continue to have trials. The so-called "Confessions of Jeremiah" are a manifestation of these struggles. They are a speech of the heart between God and the prophet (11:18–12:16; 15:10–21; 17:12–18; 18:18–23; 20:7–18). Their message is multiple. As a prophet, Jeremiah was taken by God's grace and had faith in God. As a man of his nation and time, he gave free vent to his inquiry, "Why did it happen to me? How could the Lord permit His prophet to meet such opposition, such suffering?" The answer he received was simple: abandon yourself in dedicated labor to the Lord. Sternest discipline this!

Let it not be thought that Jeremiah was a pouting churl. In the midst of the psychological torments described in his confessions and the physical sufferings described in Chapters 37–45, he wrote a book of consolations, Chapters 30 and 31. Therein is the description of the New Covenant — one of the most profound passages of the Old Testament (31:31–34). The New Covenant will be primarily with the individual. Its nature will be internal, not the Law written on tablets. Fidelity will be guaranteed because of the loving knowledge imparted to man by God of Himself in this eternal covenant.

Jeremiah was a prophet who suffered with, and died for, his people. He was an intermediary between them and God — a lonely man who had given up all for the sake of his calling.

EZEKIEL

The prophet Ezekiel was a priest who had been taken into exile to Babylon in March, 597 B.C. His task was preponderous. He was sent by God to save His people from total annihilation after a destruction God Himself would bring. The people met him with consummate pride. Before the fall of Jerusalem to the Babylonian forces in 597, pride evinced itself in overconfidence. "The temple, the temple; we have the temple." After the fall, pride raised its hydra head of despair. Few humans would have been so naturally apt to cope with these situations as the psychologically strange Ezekiel.

He answered the false confidence and the despair by telling the people, "These things come about that all may know that the Lord is God." And his forty-eight chapters make it clear that if the people accept the Lord as God they will overcome both overconfidence and despair.

His book is divided into two sections before the fall of Jerusalem. In 1:1–3:21, we have Ezekiel's call and commission. In 3:22–24:27, we have his warnings against Judah.

After the destruction of Jerusalem and the Temple, pride was shown in despair. Before the fall, Ezekiel had presented salvation history, had condemned idolatry, cultic sins, and the forgetting of the statues and ordinances of the priests. After the fall, Ezekiel taught that the Lord is still the universal God to counteract the pagan notion that when the nation fell, its god fell. Seven nations shall know that the Lord is God, when they meet their deserved punishment (25:1–32:32). Israel must hope in a glorious future; then, it will have a covenant of peace (33:1–39:29). The new Israel with its new Torah or Law, new Temple, and divine blessings will rise from the death of the old Israel (40:1–48:35). Thus pride of despair is out of place in the face of the Lord of hope.

Coarse enough to speak of human excrement, bold enough to use earthy expressions, the Ezekiel who met the overconfident would never attract men to himself — but to God.

A prophet who could not be weighed down by human failings (sin) nor even by apparent divine failures (the fall of Jerusalem) was Ezekiel. His appreciation of sin was all-embracing, profound, and realistic; but his appreciation of the omnipotence of the loving, transcendent Lord could and did buoy up a fallen, sinful nation. Yes, let the exiles, the lost Israelites, not stop with Ezekiel — but turn to the Lord.

Ezekiel's task was preponderous. His suffering was commensurate — no usual mourning for his wife, no honor of being a prophet, no talking as a prophet until the Lord stirred him. His only hope was of a reward of "life."

SECOND ISAIAH

(Cf. p. 61 above.) Chapters 40–55 of Isaiah are dated about 540 B.C. They are the work of an anonymous poet living near the end of the Babylonian exile, and the theology of these chapters is profound.

Second Isaiah's deep penetration of history and divine reality is cast in the literary form of myth, as defined on page 9 f. above. He sees the beginning as effecting the present and the future. The "first things" are the "new things." The Exodus of yore is the new Exodus of 540 B.C., but with a deeper and worldwide soteriological implication. The Lord's purpose in the beginning is now being revealed by word and deed.

Indeed, the future will see a new creation, based on the old Exodus. Within this section come the great messianic oracles known as the Songs of the Servant (42:1–4; 49:1–7; 50:4–9; 52:13–53:12). The Servant of the Lord is a man of singularly eminent virtue, a man of suffering and humiliation. The nature of the liberation is the justification of mankind, its freedom from the bondage of sin, and its introduction into a new spiritual age of mankind.

Chapters 52:13–53:12 so detail the suffering of the Servant, perhaps in the literal sense the Messiah, that they justly have been entitled the "Passion of our Lord Jesus Christ according to Isaiah." Whether literal or fuller sense, for a psychological insight of the vicarious and willing suffering of Jesus of Nazareth, they have no equal in the Old or New Testaments.

OBADIAH

Obadiah, writing in the fifth century B.C., penned twenty-one verses on the approaching fall of Edom. Edom had gloated at, and aided in, the fall of Judah. Now God's judgment fell upon this sinful nation. And the Edomites "shall drink and swallow, and shall become as though they had not been" (16b).

THIRD ISAIAH

(Cf. p. 61 above.) Chapters 56–66 of the Book of Isaiah teach that Israel's messianic future is assured. The author insists sharply on right and justice in a way not inferior to that of the preexilic prophets. This insistence is especially true of his prophetic criticism of empty, cultic activity in comparison to which social charity would be much more profitable (Is 58:1 ff.).

HAGGAI AND ZECHARIAH

Haggai and Zechariah are two prophets who together were instrumental in getting the temple rebuilt in Jerusalem between 520 and 515 B.C., after the people had been allowed to return to their land under Cyrus the Great. They see the restoration of the temple as a step in the coming glorious Day of the Lord.

JOEL

About the same time, or during the following century, a prophet named Joel proclaimed that the Day of the Lord was at hand. This vivid little book contains many ideas we have already seen in the prophets: sin, punishment, need for repentance, God's willingness to bless locally and universally. The promise of the universal donation of the Lord's power — the spirit's being poured forth on all the people in the messianic era — is a unique contribution. Sorrow for sin, certainty of triumph, and a realization of the Spirit whom we have should be our gain from a study of Joel.

MALACHI

Perhaps written about 450 B.C., the Book of Malachi is directed against the abuses within the community itself: against priests who are careless in rites and teaching; against divorces; and, above all, against a spirit of weariness and religious skepticism.

In two places (2:17–3:5 and 3:13–21), Malachi speaks

of God's eschatological activity. The Lord will undeniably come, bringing judgment on the godless and "the sun of justice with its healing rays" on those who fear him.

The book is singular in foretelling the messenger who will precede the Lord's coming. Elijah will come to melt the hearts of fathers and children. The book is immortal for its promise of the pleasing victim, the pure sacrifice: "For from the rising of the sun, even to its setting, my name is great among the nations; and everywhere they bring sacrifice to my name, and a pure offering; for great is my name among the nations, says the Lord of hosts" (1:10 f.).

JONAH

Jonah is one of the best known books of the Old Testament. It was written about the fifth century, when nationalistic exclusivism on the part of the Jerusalem priesthood had become very strong. It sought to remind the new community of the restored exiles that the love of God was broader than they were conceiving it. God had not chosen Israel to play favorites but to be the bearer of His saving power to all.

The literary form of Jonah is not history but an allegorical parable. Jonah is portrayed as a prophet in Palestine who hears the command of the Lord to become an instrument of mercy to the city which was the worst enemy of his people, Nineveh, the capital of Assyria. Refusing to carry out the Lord's command, he flees in the opposite direction by boat as fast as he can go. But the Lord will not let him get away. God has him swallowed by a big fish which spews him up again on the shore of Palestine, where he is once again commanded to go to Nineveh.

The city of Nineveh, after having had the proclamation to repent preached to it, wholeheartedly repents so that God does not have to punish it by destruction. This disgusts Jonah. He quotes one of the great confessions of God's love in the Old Testament, namely, that God is merciful and gracious and slow to anger and full of mercy, and uses that precisely as his own excuse for anger (4:2). In other words, the mercy of God is a fine thing when it is directed to Jonah's own people, but a disgusting thing when directed toward his enemies.

The theological teaching of Jonah is profound: a satire on the chauvinism of the Jews; God's providence, omnipotence, and mercy extends to all men. It is a commentary on Ezekiel 33:11, "As I live says the Lord God, I swear I take no pleasure in the death of the wicked man, but rather in the wicked man's conversion, that he may live" (cf. also Ez 18:23; Jer 18:8). God wills the salvation of all men — as pointed a lesson now as then.

With Malachi and Joel, the prophets of the Old Testament are silenced. Watching, not warning, becomes the byword.

God tried to rescue His people from His punishing hand. He gave the corporate body a conscience. This conscience dictated the "here and now" of the covenant's applications. The people must be just. Judges should not demand bribes for releasing the innocent. The poor should not be sold into slavery. Israelites should not act as "cannibals." The conscience spoke in figures of speech that are electrifying even in our time and our language.

The conscience had so to speak since its judgment came from such strong and varied personalities as the lover Hosea, the domineering Amos, the nearly psychopathic Ezekiel, the poet Isaiah, and even the timid and faltering Jeremiah. The prophets are interesting just from the characters whose ideas they bring to the fore.

Their condemnation of bribery, adultery, chicanery, reliance on power instead of on the Lord is as pointed for tendencies in American capitalism, conformity and militarism as it was for the Jews of the eighth to the fifth century before Christ. Their message is timely. More important, their message about the mercy of God attempting to bring back His beloved Israel to its chosen pact with Him remains timeless. For who could suspect it, were it not revealed?

CHAPTER SIX

THE SANCTIFYING WORD

God's Prayers, the Psalms

THE psalms are prayers. In their verses, a man acknowledges his need for God, He trusts in God. He confides in God. The psalms contain the four generic reasons of all prayer: adoration, petition, reparation, and thanksgiving.

Here we hope to share with you our love for the psalms. To do so we will briefly explain the social milieu, literary form, teaching, numbering, and "Davidic" authorship of these Jewish poems. Lastly, you will find the main theme of each psalm. By detailing this main theme, we hope to encourage you to pray God's prayers.

The exact social situation in which most of the psalms originated is now unknown, as is their date of composition. Many of them were certainly used in the worship of the community. By them, Israel petitioned God, thanked Him, expressed its hope in Him, and loved Him.

Scholars have divided the psalms according to diverse literary forms. In turn these literary forms may be subordinated to three of the four purposes of every prayer. The psalms, cast in the literary form of hymns or songs of praise to the Lord-King or in honor of the fidelity of God, are prayers of adoration. These psalms adoring God contain teachings about sacred history, the covenant, and the splendid manifestations of God's presence called theophanies.

Psalms in the literary form of lament are prayers of petition. They teach or presuppose the teaching that after life there is nothing except Sheol — a place of senseless existence (cf. p. 87 f.). You will find curses in them, damning God's enemy. This is as Christian a sentiment about the devil and

God's unrepentant enemies as any (cf. similar principles in notion of *kerem,* p. 50 f.)! You will find psalms about men who are tormented by suffering, psalms of trust, and psalms blessing others.

Psalms in the literary form of thanksgiving hymns express gratitude to Almighty God. The cause of the gratitude is frequently God's mercy in forgiving sin.

Some of the literary forms proposed by scholars do not easily fit under one or other of the classical ends of prayer. The "wisdom psalms" are more instructions in a prudent way of life than prayers. "Royal psalms" and "psalms of Zion" (Jerusalem) contain praise, petition, and thanksgiving in about equal measure.

Written by poets, the psalms love the concrete, the down-to-earth. Written by Jews, the psalms mirror Jewish history which is our religious heritage. Written by Semites, the psalms use parallelism, i.e., one part of a verse frequently says the same thing as the second part.

Both the Hebrew and the Latin Bibles contain 150 psalms, although the same material is divided differently in the two Bibles so as to reach the number 150. The Protestant Bible follows the Hebrew numbering; the Catholic, the Latin. The respective numberings are:

Hebrew	Latin
1–8	1–8
9–10	9
11–113	10–112
114–115	113
116	114–115
117–146	116–145
147	146–147
148–150	148–150

In content, however, there are only 147 distinct psalms. Psalm 13 (Latin) is identical with Psalm 52 save for the name used for God. Psalm 69 is identical with Psalm 39:14–

18. Psalm 107 is simply a combination of Psalm 56:8–12 and Psalm 39:8–14.

Of these psalms, seventy-three are ascribed to David in the Hebrew text, and he undoubtedly wrote some of these. Many are attributed to him because David was in the eyes of the Hebrews, the musician par excellence.

The authors of the psalms have expressed every sentiment of the human heart. The emotional quality of the psalms ranges from love to hatred, from thanksgiving to cursing, from blessing to revenge, from humble begging of God to shouting that He do something. Whether contemplating in majestic appreciation God's wonder or beckoning the Drunken Warrior, the psalms answer every desire of the human soul. In joy and sorrow, in acts of thanksgiving and petition, requesting forgiveness and manifesting innocence, in any state of mind a man can find his solace and accompaniment in the 150 psalms of the Old Testament.

In the following pages, we list the literary form and the main theme of each of the psalms. Make the psalms your own personal prayers. Use the main theme to help you find what solace you need at a particular moment. Then you are using God's prayers as a personal encounter with Him.

Psalm No.	Literary Form	Main Theme
1	Wisdom	Joy is in good, not evil, deeds.
2	Royal	God's king will win.
3	Confidence	Trust in God alone.
4	Confidence	Peace is found only in trusting in God alone.
5	Lament	God is holy; He will grant the needy joy.
6	Lament	A sinner hopes because of God's pity and loving-kindness.
7	Lament	God: condemn the guilty!
8	Hymn	Awe at God's nature revealed in creation — especially man.
9A	Thanks	God's act of justice.
9B	Lament	From malicious enemies, deliver me.
10	Confidence	Trust, even when pillars are cast down.

Psalm No.	Literary Form	Main Theme
11	Unknown	May God deliver from the proud! Amen!
12	Lament	Prayer of an afflicted lover of God.
13	Wisdom	Joy because the atheist will be punished.
14	Wisdom	Love of neighbor is love of God, which brings His friendship.
15	Trust	Communion with God is my unique good.
16	Lament	God protects against any enemy.
17	Thanks	A contemplation of God in the covenantly guaranteed act of protecting the king.
18	Hymn	Awe of the Lord begets holiness and health.
19	Royal	God — not chariots — assures victory.
20	Royal	Thanks to God who has blessed the king.
21	Lament	Forsaken yet saved by God; glory to Him!
22	Trust	My eternal Friend: God!
23	Unknown	God, Lord of Hosts.
24	Lament	A sinner trusts God to give His friendship, i.e., instruction, guidance, pardon, fidelity.
25	Lament	I wash in innocence; keep me thus!
26:1–6	Confidence	Effects of God's presence: peace of mind and holy abandonment.
26:7–14	Lament	Help me a sinner, now and always.
27	Lament	There but for the grace of God go I.
28	Hymn	God's glory in the tempest.
29	Thanks	Humility reverses the pride that went before the fall.
30	Lament	The meaning of suffering: cling only to God.
31	Thanks	Happiness of return to friendship with God.
32	Hymn	Awe before God's reliable word.
33	Thanks	Taste and see how good the Lord is to the needy.
34	Lament	Prayer to achieve trust in God.
35	Wisdom — Hymn	Man without God is nothing; God: continue giving your friends life and light!

Psalm No.	Literary Form	Main Theme
36	*Collection of proverbs in which an old man teaches trust in justice.*	
37	*Lament*	A repentant sinner trusts in God, even in great sufferings.
38	*Lament*	What avail a vaporous life under God's wrath? Please, some respite!
39	*Thanks — Lament*	God, as before, do all!
40	*Thanks — Lament*	Thanks after sickness.
41 and 42	*Lament*	I shall go unto God's altar for joy to be given to me, His suffering exile.
43	*Lament*	Why does God permit Israel, His beloved, to suffer? God, help!
44	*Royal*	Marriage of the just king with his devoted and gifted spouse.
45	*Zion*	Fear of danger? Not with the God of hosts.
46	*The Lord-King*	Awe at God, Creator, Conserver, King.
47	*Hymn*	The Lord-King is Israel's enduring strength.
48	*Wisdom*	Death levels all. God will give life.
49	*God's fidelity*	I am the Lord, your God; Sincerely offer sacrifice to live.
50	*Lament*	I detest all my sins because they offend Thee, my God.
51	*Wisdom*	To ruin with the liar; to God with the just — these are facts!
52	*Wisdom*	Joy because atheist will be punished.
53	*Lament*	Help in mortal danger.
54	*Lament*	When evil has all, even a friend, still trust in God.
55	*Lament*	In God I trust without fear.
56	*Lament*	In my persecution, be glorified, O Lord.
57	*Lament*	In God's vindication of official injustice the just will glory.
58	*Lament*	Surrounded by mongrels, I confidently sing to God.
59	*Lament*	Even when God has apparently rejected us, trust only in His promise.
60	*Lament*	Suffering occasions trust and prayer.
61	*Trust*	Peace — only in God.
62	*Confidence*	God, my life.

Psalm No.	Literary Form	Main Theme
63	*Lament*	Trust God, punisher of evildoers.
64	*Hymn*	For harvest, all: praise to the Omnipotent.
65	*Hymn*	Thanks to the Omnipotent, even in trials.
66	*Hymn*	May all joyfully obey the God of blessings.
67	*Hymn*	God's epiphany means punishment for the evil and glory for the good. Come!
68	*Lament — Thanks*	In anguish, trust.
69	*Lament*	God, to my aid — quickly!
70	*Lament*	Experience teaches: trust in the Almighty Friend — no matter what!
71	*Royal*	Thy Kingdom come!
72	*Wisdom*	The just will live by loyalty, even in the face of scandal.
73	*Lament*	How long until salvation, O Lord?
74	*The Lord-King*	The Creator is still in charge.
75	*Zion*	The Lord-Victor, yesterday, today, forever!
76	*Lament*	The Lord, the invisible and redeeming God of the Reed Sea, has not changed.
77	*Wisdom*	Your sins can lose you your election.
78	*Lament*	Lord, You owe it to Yourself to avenge Yours.
79	*Lament*	Save Your believing nation, which You in Your enigmatic wisdom destroyed.
80	*God's fidelity*	In oppression, praise God who will give salvation to fidelity.
81	*Lament*	God will punish evil. Amen.
82	*Lament*	God: rout Your enemies.
83	*Zion*	I would rather spend one day with God than 1000 elsewhere.
84	*Hymn*	Loyalty will bring joy and salvation.
85	*Lament*	Lord, be Master!
86	*Zion*	Mother Jerusalem's conception of revelation gives birth to God's one family.
87	*Lament*	Without hope, I prayed to You, my God.
88	*Royal*	When will Your Davidic throne take the place of Your present anger?

Psalm No.	Literary Form	Main Theme
89	*Lament*	What can dust say to the Mountain? Help!
90	*Confidence*	God, my sure Protector.
91	*Thanks*	God's past just deeds guarantee future justice both to bad and to good.
92	*The Lord-King*	Awe at God, King of material and moral world.
93	*Wisdom*	The Creator-Avenger can and must chastise evil and reward good.
94	*God's fidelity*	Awe of God, Creator of the supernatural.
95	*The Lord-King*	Awe to God, Author of Sacred History.
96	*The Lord-King*	The Day of the Lord.
97	*The Lord-King*	Let all rejoice in the saving King.
98	*The Lord-King*	Holy, Holy, Holy!
99	*Hymn*	Awe of God's fatherly care of Israel.
100	*Royal*	The piety of a ruler under God.
101	*Lament*	Trust in the Lord, who loves His people!
102	*Hymn — Thanks*	Holy God, I a sinner, praise Your name.
103	*Hymn*	Your creatures follow Your purpose.
104	*God's fidelity*	I love my God, who kept His part of my salvation's bargain!
105	*God's fidelity*	Our sins are always before us. Spare!
106	*Thanks — Hymn*	Awed thanks to God for saving man.
107	*Lament*	Trust for victory, even in apparently defeated people.
108	*Lament*	Thanks to God for surely damning the unrepentant sinner.
109	*Royal*	God's triumphant king-priest!
110	*Hymn*	Awe at God's revelation-in-act.
111	*Wisdom*	Joy in obedience and charity.
112	*Hymn*	Almighty God loves the needy.
113A	*Hymn*	Myth of God's choosing and saving Israel.
113B	*God's fidelity*	God, not idols, blesses.
114	*Thanks*	The peace of a beloved lover of God.
115	*Thanks*	What can I return for all He gave me?
116	*Hymn*	Awe of God who will bless all because of His covenant with Israel.
117	*Thanks*	Thank God for His constancy.

Psalm No.	Literary Form	Main Theme
118	*Lament, etc.*	May the psalmist's Friend hear his plea.
119	*Lament*	Thanks for safety from the barbarian.
120	*Unknown*	Your Shield is the author and conserver of Sacred History.
121	*Zion*	Peace for Jerusalem!
122	*Lament*	Despised Israel looks to its Lord with reverential trust.
123	*Thanks*	Our help is in name of the Lord who made all.
124	*Lament*	May Israel's faith not falter.
125	*Unknown*	May grace through death become glory.
126	*Wisdom*	Without Me, you can do nothing.
127	*Wisdom*	Oh the joy of the pious married couple!
128	*Thanks*	Tribulations have a divinely set limit; cursed be their causers.
129	*Lament*	From Sheol of sin to trust in God the Savior.
130	*Trust*	Humility.
131	*Royal*	On account of David, let Israel reign.
132	*Wisdom*	How beautiful the blessing which is charity.
133	*Unknown*	Good-bye to the Temple.
134	*Hymn*	Praise to the God of Creation and Redemption.
135	*Hymn*	Awe to God's piety in Sacred History and harvest.
136	*Zion*	Curse the impenitent ridiculers of the Lord's wisdom and power.
137	*Thanks*	Thank You! Take care of Your part in my future.
138	*Wisdom*	God — all-knowing, everywhere, and omnificent — make me holy.
139	*Lament*	Protect me from my unjust enemies.
140	*Lament*	Keep me from giving in to temptation.
141	*Lament*	God, help Your abandoned prisoner.
142	*Lament*	A penitent: only God can give life.
143	*Royal*	Happy the people whom the Lord assures of salvation.
144	*Hymn*	I will bless the Lord forever.
145	*Hymn*	Happy trust in the Lord — unique, omnipotent, and loyal lover of the needy.

Psalm No.	Literary Form	Main Theme
146	*Hymn*	Awe to the wise Almighty who cares for the helpless.
147	*Hymn*	Awe before God's gift of peace to Israel.
148	*Hymn*	Heaven and earth: praise God's name.
149	*Hymn*	Let Israel show God's presence in sword and song.
150	*Hymn*	You: praise the Lord.

CHAPTER SEVEN

THE WORD OF CONSOLATION

Hope in Disillusion

THE preexilic prophets threatened punishment if sin continued. The postexilic prophets tried to solace the people. The Babylonian Exile (587–539 B.C.) is a pivot in God's relation with the people of His covenant.

This chapter will sketch Israel's history during the few years immediately before, and the centuries after, the Exile. We will see what new relation in God's pact with Israel resulted. We will also introduce you to the inspired books from this period.

Sin caused the Exile. About 200 B.C., the author of Baruch gave his pious reflections on the Exile. The author dramatized sin, confessed sin, turned from sin, and looked for salvation. Baruch 1–5 viewed life as a drama whose actors were the finite sinner and the Infinite Good. The sinner sinned and searched salvation in the wisdom given by God. (Baruch 6 is a separate work which ridicules polytheism and confesses God.)

On page 51 ff. above, we detailed the sins which caused the fall of the northern kingdom of Israel. Pro-Egyptian factions quarreled with pro-Assyrian. In 732 B.C. the Assyrian King Sargon made the king of Israel his puppet (cf. 2 Kgs 15:10–30). Yet the kingdom of Israel failed to learn its lesson and rebelled, only to be conquered again in 721 B.C. (cf 2 Kgs 17). More than 27,000 Israelites of the upper social class were deported. This number is learned from the annals of the Assyrian King Sargon. He imported other peoples to replace the deportees. In exile the people of the northern tribes slowly lost their own individuality. God's warned punishment had come.

The Southern Kingdom of Judah fared little better. It maintained a token of independence for one hundred and fifty years longer than the North. In 587 B.C., the pro-Egyptian party took over. In 586 B.C., the Babylonian King Nebuchadnezzar despoiled Judah, sacking Jerusalem, destroying the Temple (2 Kgs 18–24; 2 Ch 33–36; Jer 39:4–7). God's promised land was in the hands of foreigners. By the covenant, had not God promised a land and a people? Was the covenant at long last finished?

Was the covenant over? A paradox occurs in Sacred History. On the one hand, it seems that the covenant is over since never again will Israel have real independence. On the other hand, Israel did receive God's help to rebuild the temple and Jerusalem's walls. God's grace aided them to a deeper appreciation of the law. God gave them inspired books. How to solve the paradox of a God who continues blessing His faithless wife? The solution is that the gifts were no longer bestowed because of the Sinaitic covenantal union. Rather, they were granted to fulfill the promises to Abraham and David. The five hundred years after the Exile were a period of purification for the new and eternal covenant in Jesus, Abraham's descendant and David's offspring.

We, you and I, can see this meaning in the postexilic sufferings. Not so the Jew in 539 B.C. Released from exile under the benign Cyrus the Persian, the Jew returned to disillusion. Instead of an expected time of peace and prosperity the Jew met unfriendly people and hunger. A contemporary of this era, the author of Lamentations has caught its funereal spirit. He composed a dirge over the misery of Jerusalem, the divine judgment upon the city. Praying for mercy, he never lost faith in God, the Lord of all events who acts justly in even the most tragic. His confession of faith included an act of contrition and ended with an act of hope in the God of mercy.

Lamentations taught contrition. A compiler, called the Chronicler, urged hope. God's goodness, from the very beginning, prepared for David. Punishment had come because of sins, especially those of the kings. The messianic blessings promised to David would be fulfilled if the people were faithful to God's worship and the law (1 and 2 Chronicles).

It took twenty years to build the comparatively unimposing new temple. Another forty years had to pass before the walls of Jerusalem gave security. Was this the glorious restoration promised by the prophets? (Cf. Ezr 3:1–6:22 and the Book of Nehemiah.)

Security was indeed what the returned exiles needed. And they found it in the law of the Lord. A man who, together with Ezekiel, may be called the father of Judaism, gave the needed encouragement. Ezra, a scribe and priest, stressed the law as that which would stabilize the nation.

Three types of literature reach their zenith in the five hundred years before Jesus: the historical novel, apocalyptic, and wisdom literature. Each, in its own way, instills hope in a man of faith.

Esther, Tobit, and Judith are historical novels. All were put into their present form between 300 and 150 B.C. All three were written to teach God's providential care, not to detail a history. The form of an historical novel is well suited to teach hope. The absence of history in the novel teaches that faith, once historically believable, needs no more proof. God's promise must be believed.

Esther is the suspenseful drama of the near liquidation of the Jews in Persia. God had made the Jewess, Esther, the Persian Queen, and thereby laid the basis to thwart the pogrom. Moreover the pogrom is turned on the unjust enemy — occasioned by a providential act of the Jew, Mordechai, in saving the king's life. God provides for His own, is the teaching of the novel Esther. In Him, hope!

Judith is the symbolic story of a woman's killing a general. A huge army under General Holofernes was sent to punish the rebellious Jews. Making his successful way through Palestine, Holofernes was seduced by Judith. She plied him drunk with wine and cut off his head. Judith teaches God's providence: He can use even a woman to conquer the strength of an apparently irresistible enemy. In Him, hope!

Tobit also teaches God's providence. God changed suffering to joy. A displaced Jew, the elder Tobit, practiced true piety to God and God's people. But Tobit became blind and poverty-stricken. Moreover a relative of his was seemingly cursed; Sarah had seven husbands die on her marriage nights. God's providence, personified in Archangel Raphael, led the younger Tobias through dangers to bring money and health to his father and happily to marry Sarah. God has changed sorrow to happiness. Hope in Him!

The Book of Daniel also taught hope in God by example. In 1:1–6:29 and 13:1–14:42, God blesses and protects the good Daniel in all his needs.

The rest of Daniel taught a like message of hope, based on Israel's previous history. But this message was couched in a strange use of symbols, enigmatic numbers, and catastrophic happenings. This mysterious way of teaching hope through past history is called the apocalyptic literary form. This form was common in Jewish literature of postexilic times. Daniel, the Apocalypse of the New Testament, and the eschatological discourses in the first three Gospels are the clearest examples in the Bible.

The Book of Daniel was composed by an unknown author about 165 B.C. The Jews were being persecuted by the Seleucids and hope was essential. Open teaching that the Jews would one day defeat the Seleucids would have been treason. The enigma of the apocalypse hid the treason. That literary form inculcated hope based on past experience. In 7:1–28, the author of Daniel uses four beasts to symbolize the four kingdoms of Babylonia, Mede, Persia, and Greece. These four have been or will be replaced by Israel, symbolized by the Son of Man. Let the persecuted Jews hope.

In 8:1–27, the vision of the he-goat (Alexander the Great) defeating the ram (Persian-Median empire) occurs. The horn of the he-goat had been broken into the four rulers that divided Alexander's empire at his death. One of these (the Seleucid dynasty) attacks the people of God. After a determined short time, this "horn" too will be demolished. Again, hope even in persecution is the teaching.

Chapter 9 presents the well-known vision of seventy weeks of years. Using the apocalyptic literary form, the author intends no precise numerical prophecy. The symbol of the seventy weeks of years teaches that Israel's sins have merited a long time of persecution. The persecution has almost run its course. Thus, again, hope. Chapters 10 to 12 give the vision of a great war. A resplendent man explains to Daniel that history is governed by God. After death, a resurrection to a joyful life awaits the good (12:1–3). Suffering will be a short duration. Hope for the future, based on God's love in the past, is the message of Daniel.

Along with the historical novel and the apocalyptic literary form, this era saw the perfection of the wisdom literature. Under the influence of the Hellenists, this literature, long in existence, reached its acme. The books of wisdom — Proverbs, Job, Ecclesiastes (Coheleth), Sirach, and Wisdom — are among the most tantalizing and the most frustrating of Old Testament literature. They tantalize because they ask questions everyone wishes answered. They frustrate because, lacking a knowledge of Christ, they only partially answer their own questions.

The wise man sought the prudent way of living. He asked, "How can man live rightly?" "Why is there suffering?" "How can man be happy?" "Why does God test men?" To compare the attitude of each book, we will trace one question, "Why be good?"

Proverbs optimistically replies that goodness will be rewarded in this life. Its pithy answers all presuppose the Old Testament notion of reward in this life.

But facts do not bear out this answer. Experience teaches that the good do suffer. Job acknowledges the suffering of the good and responds, "The Lord gives and the Lord takes away. Blessed be the name of the Lord." Ecclesiastes sees all human values as "Vanity of vanities and all is vanity."

Sirach does not go along with the pessimist. He interprets the former books of the Old Testament midrashically (cf. p. 9) to show that the good will prosper in this life. Only Wisdom knows that "There is immortality in kinship with Wisdom" (8:17) and has thus a convincing reason to be good.

We now introduce each of the five wisdom books.

PROVERBS

Compiled about 400 B.C., the Book of Proverbs is a compendium of perhaps five centuries of sayings. Its attribution to Solomon, Agur, and Lamuel is probably due to the fact that these were men of great wisdom of yore. The first nine chapters set a religious aspect to the whole book. Wisdom and Dame Folly are personified. Dame Folly may be a real woman living in Israel. If so, she invites Israelite youth to a cult banquet which is accompanied by illicit relations. Folly is opposed to Wisdom. Wisdom's allurements can and should ultimately win.

Proverbs 10:1–31:31, for the most part, contains proverbs — capsules of the experiences of years. The proverb has application only in a concrete, determined experience. It is not of universal extension. A proverb deals in the past, not the future. Its truth will be known only after a similar experience. A cursory look at Proverbs will convince you that it is well worth reading, "Apply your heart to instruction; and your ears to words of knowledge" (23:12).

JOB

A very tentative date for Job is the fifth century B.C. Tennyson wrote that Job was "the greatest poem of ancient and modern times." For us its main interest is its probing search into the problem of suffering and God's justice. Job shows that his (and our) contemporaries' explanations of suffering are inadequate. They say that suffering is a judgment for sin, a warning to avoid a heavier punishment. Suffering purifies (3:1–37:24). All of these notions are too shallow.

In 38–42, Job comes face to face with the transcendent and immanent presence of God. He then realizes more and more that God's work in the universe is too deep for man to understand. God's love is too great to fathom. Man can never fully understand the problem of suffering.

And yet, in 42:7, God tells Job that he was right and his friends were wrong. As the book now exists, the judgment in 42:7 is the inspired judgment that Job was correct in questioning. This means that a man may ask God, "Why is there suffering?" One may realize the seeming contradiction between suffering and God's love, may question God — never wavering in his faith. It is, in other words, greater faith to see the question, to ask it, and to remain loyal than to ignore the problem.

Faith and loyalty do not allow a man to waver even when he questions. Only when a man questions and believes has he truly begun to plummet the abyss of suffering — so teaches Job.

COHELETH (ECCLESIASTES)

A conjectured date of Ecclesiastes is 300 B.C. The author takes all that man finds dear, puts it to the cleaver of skepticism and teaches, "Vanity of vanities and all is vanity." Nothing of life — work, joy, wealth, marriage, fame — nothing escapes his scrutinizing eye. And all of it, "Vanity!" His judgment is severe, yet true, if only it leads to the only ground for hope in God and His Incarnate Word, but about the latter Coheleth did not know enough.

The author is a pessimist. Still he teaches that, while all

is vanity, life is worth the living. "Anything you can turn
your hand to, do with what power you have; for there will
be no work, nor reason, nor knowledge, nor wisdom in the
nether world where you are going" (9:10; cf. 5:17–19).
Not hedonistic, but realistic, the author could do nothing
better with the limited revelation at his disposal. Christianity
takes the vacuity that *Coheleth* would make and tells us that
Christ fills all of life's nothingness.

SIRACH (ECCLESIASTICUS)

About 180 B.C., Jesus, grandson of Sirach, composed a
vivid message on a variety of subjects. Keeping within the
tradition of the former books of the Old Testament more
than the previous wisdom books Sirach's sincerity is his
greatest claim to literary fame. Of the matters treated, these
are especially developed and easily profitable: friends and
friendship (6:5–17; 9:10–16; 11:29–34; 13:1–25; 36:18–
37:15); speech (5:11–6:1; 19:5–16); providence (2:1–11;
18:1–13); woman and marriage (9:1–9; 25:1–26:18; 36:-
21–27; 42:9–14).

The answer that Sirach gave to the evils in the world was
that man's sin caused them, even death (15:11–20; 39:12–
35; 41:1–13). Since death comes to all, use your wealth for
your own happiness and that of your neighbor (14:3–19).
Happiness is given especially to Israel which has God's Wisdom: God's Law (Ch. 24).

WISDOM (WISDOM OF SOLOMON)

Composed by one author, not Solomon, in about 100 B.C.,
Wisdom developed the idea of a blessed immortality (1:1–
5:16). Until this period, the Old Testament's notion of the
afterlife, for just and sinful alike, was a place of existence
without sense experience, called Sheol, Hades, or the Nether
World. More than Daniel (cf. p. 84) or 2 Maccabees (cf.
89), the author unfolded the significance of a happy eternity.
The wise man, synonymous in Wisdom with the good, will

be happy forever. Suffering has more sense: God gives it to
man to make him wise and thus prepare him for a happy
immortality (3:1–8). Examples of God's wise men in the
Old Testament encourage wisdom (10:1–19:22, *passim*).
The author's personification of Wisdom (7:22–8:1, etc.)
prepares for the personality of the Word in John's Gospel.

Three other books were written in this period: the Canticle
of Canticles, and the two books called Maccabees.

THE CANTICLES OF CANTICLES

Probably written around 300 B.C., the Canticle depicts
pure, conjugal love. The literary form is disputed. We prefer
the drama. The Canticle has been the source of many mystics'
contemplative love of God.

The Canticle portrays the love of man for woman in deepest symbolism. The following selection will permit the reader
to savor its magnificence, "For stern as death is love, relent-
less as the nether world is devotion. . . . Deep waters cannot
quench love, nor floods sweep it away. Were one to offer all
he owns to purchase love, he would be roundly mocked"
(8:6 f.).

1 AND 2 MACCABEES

The Jews had undergone a severe persecution by the
Syrians from 175 to 142 B.C. The first Book of Maccabees,
written about 90 B.C., is in general a statistical history of the
persecution. Its wars and heroes, especially the Maccabee
boys, make thrilling reading.

The second Book of Maccabees, written around 124 B.C.,
recounts the same persecution until 160 B.C. Its literary form
is "pathetic history," events narrated to move its reader to
sympathy for the persecuted. Its main teaching is that no
compromise can be permitted between Judaism and Hellen-
ism. God's glory is achieved in the death of Jewish martyrs
(2 Mach 3:38; 7:37; 10:7; 12:23; 15:34).

There are important individual teachings in 2 Maccabees:

the resurrection of the dead (7:9; 14:46); sanctions after death (6:26); a prayer for the dead (12:41–46); and the intercession of the saints (15:12–16).

With the second Book of Maccabees, the Old Testament closes. More than five hundred years of a people's living have passed rapidly in this chapter. God wreaked a vindictive punishment on the ten tribes of the North. God purified the South through the Exile and restoration. God gave hope through the historical novels and Daniel. God inspired the wise man to query into life's problems.

The dissatisfied people learned to yearn for the promised salvation. The culmination of their longing was born in 6 or 7 B.C. in Bethlehem. The legalists among the Jews would never recognize Him. The wise men would stumble over His crucifixion. The apocalyptists would yet be looking years after the Longed-For of the ages had come and gone. The Christian would believe in "Christ-Jesus who has become for us God-given wisdom, and justice, and sanctification, and redemption" (1 Cor 1:30)!

CHAPTER EIGHT

THE FAITHFUL WORD

God's Fatherly Love (Hosea 11–14)

UNTIL we begin to read the Bible, all study about it will remain sterile. One of the most beautiful parts of the Old Testament is Hosea 11–14. These chapters teach that God, the father of Israel, must punish His disobedient child. His love will somehow make this punishment medicinal.

God's love is described in the most tender of terms:

> When Israel was a child I loved him,
>   out of Egypt I called my son.
>
>   (11:1)
>
> It was I who taught Ephraim to walk,
>   who took them in my arms;
> I drew them with human cords,
>   with bands of love;
> I fostered them like one
>   who raises an infant to his cheeks.
>
>   (11:3 f.)

The above verses need no explanation. When a mob was in slavery in Egypt, God formed it into Israel — into His son Israel. He instructed Ephraim (a name for the Northern Kingdom) in the rudiments of the infant — how to walk. All was done under as gentle an impulse as love.

For His love, God was repaid with sin. Idolatry, trust in foreign powers, and social injustice became rampant. Ungrateful payment of God's friendship!

> The more I called them,
>   the farther they went from me,
> Sacrificing to the Baals
>   and burning incense to idols.
>
>   (11:2)

> Ephraim has surrounded me with lies,
> the house of Israel with deceit;
> Juda is still rebellious against God,
> against the Holy One, who is faithful.
> Ephraim chases the wind,
> ever pursuing the gale.
> His lies and falsehoods are many:
> he comes to terms with Assyria,
> and carries oil to Egypt.
>
> (12:1 f.)

Israel's ingratitude was in direct proportion to God's favor. She offered worship to the gods of the day, the Baals. Moreover, trusting in Egypt and Assyria, she sent gifts to them to gain their help. Paradoxically, this seeking of these nations' benevolence would profit her as much as trying to catch the wind or put a tornado in a paper bag. Yes, foreign allies were deceitful.

Israel requited God's paternal love with mockery, trusting not in Him but in Egypt and Assyria. What could any father do except punish such a child? And God in the following verses does threaten to punish his iniquitous offspring:

> He shall return to the land of Egypt,
> And Assyria shall be his king;
> The sword shall begin with his cities
> and end by consuming his solitudes.
> Because they refused to repent,
> their own counsels shall devour them.
> His people are in suspense about returning
> to him; and God, though in unison they
> cry out to him, shall not raise them up.
>
> (11:5–7)

God shall punish Israel with a slavery similar to that of Israel in Egypt. To Assyria, they had once turned. Assyria will now devastate all of Israel's cities and towns. Thus do Israel's plans for freedom turn into slavery.

The threat of punishment continues. Israel robbed; God will send her back to living as a nomad. Out of houses and into tents will He put her:

> I am the Lord, Your God,
>> since the Land of Egypt;
> I will again have you live
>> in tents, as in that appointed time.
>
> (12:10)

Israel committed idolatry. Its altars will be as heaps of stones:

> In Galaad is falsehood, they
>> have come to nought.
> In Galgal they sacrifice to
>> bullocks;
> Their altars are like heaps
>> of stones,
> In the furrows of the field.
>
> (12:12)

Israel's crimes have merited death. This will come:

> Ephraim has exasperated his Lord;
>> therefore he shall cast his blood-
>> guilt upon him and repay him for
>> his outrage.
> Ephraim's word caused fear,
>> for he was exalted in Israel
>> but he sinned through Baal and died.
>
> (12:15; 13:1)

God's punishments are further described in 13:3 where Israel's powerlessness and oblivion are figuratively set forth, "They shall be like a morning cloud or like dew that early passes away, like chaff . . . or like smoke." Perhaps one of the most masterly expressions of the frustrations of Israel is that of the fetus that is stopped in the breach:

> The guilt of Israel is wrapped up,
>> his sin is stored away.
> The birth pangs shall come for him,
>> but he shall be an unwise child;
> For when it is time he shall not present
>> himself where children break forth.
>
> (13:12 f.)

The prophet's language is brutal, even for our age so accustomed to the inhuman:

> They shall fall by the sword,
>> their little ones shall be dashed to pieces,
>> their expectant mothers shall be ripped open.
>> (14:1)

The barbarity of the triumphant army that had besieged Samaria for three years is doubtlessly described. The sacking of God's child would be thorough.

And yet, throughout all of this, hope:

> For I am God and not man
>> the Holy One present among you!
>> I will not let the flames consume you.
>> (11:9)
>
> My heart is overwhelmed,
>> my pity is stirred.
> I will not give vent to my blazing anger,
>> I will not destroy Ephraim again.
>> (11:8 f.)

The last verses of these touching chapters are replete with promises of a new time. As always in these chapters Hosea's teaching is found all together: sin, wavering punishment, need for punishment, hope. So, also in Chapter 14 all elements are found. Hope, however, is the note on which the prophecy of Hosea ends:

> I will heal their defection,
>> I will love them freely;
>> for my wrath is turned away from them.
> I will be like the dew for Israel:
> He shall blossom like the lily.
>> (14:5 f.)

Hosea continues foreseeing the blessing of the Lord in terms of nature, the strong odiferous cedar, the magnificent olive, etc. Such will be Israel in the new times.

The God of the Old Testament is not a God of fear. How could He be when He treated this sinful son as the most tender of fathers would? Chastisement was necessary in order to purify, for the son's own happiness. And yet, even chastisement was meted out only with the due measure of a loving father over the son whom he begot, nourished, cherished, and eventually loved even to the cross.

EPILOGUE TO PART ONE

THE FULFILLMENT OF THE OLD TESTAMENT

HAS God been thwarted? Is the Old Testament not the account of God's failure? God created man and man sinned. God chose Israel and Israel sinned.

If God had created or covenanted with Israel alone in view, then God had failed! But the New Testament tells us that Jesus of Nazareth, the Messiah, was the purpose of God's creation and covenanting. He it is who gives meaning to the Old Testament. On account of Him God created and began Sacred History. Jesus of Nazareth, the only-begotten Son of God, His Word, is the reason for, and the meaning of, the Old Testament.

We now turn to the New Testament. First, we will study the life of Christ. Then, we will study each of the books which make up God's final word.

PART TWO: THE NEW TESTAMENT

CHAPTER NINE

THE WORD MADE FLESH

1. *Jesus of Nazareth, the Failure*

"AND the Word was made flesh and dwelt among us." Why? To be in person the greatest revelation God has given us, to communicate to us His intimate, personal life in the Trinity and express God's solicitude and love for mankind. "On God no man ever laid his eyes; the only-begotten Son, who rests in the Father's bosom, has himself been the interpreter" (Jn 1:18 f.). Jesus of Nazareth in His words and deeds expressed the Father. Indeed, He and the Father are one (Jn 10:30).

Thus we turn to the New Testament for our knowledge of God. God wants us to know about Him, and has actually told us about Himself and us. And we learn about the Father from and through the Son — His human life, suffering, and death. Above all, we learn of the consuming love of the Father for us, His creatures, from Jesus of Nazareth; for God so loved the world "that he gave his only-begotten Son" (Jn 3:16).

In the following pages, we will discuss the earthly life of that Jesus, as He lived and as He died. How human He appears! In stressing His sacred humanity, we seek to encourage the prayerful study of the God who became man.

The outline immediately following sketches the major events in the public life of Christ. The outline is not definitive. Scholars disagree on many issues.

OUTLINE OF OUR LORD'S PUBLIC LIFE
  I. Ministry in Judea (April and May, A.D. 28)
     1. First Pasch in Jerusalem
     2. Ministry just out of Judea
     3. In Samaria

II. Ministry in Galilee (May, 28, to April, 29)
1. The Baptist's imprisonment; beginning of Kingdom with miracles and preaching (April to June, 28)
2. Sermon on the Mount (April to June, 28)
3. Parables (November, 28, to April, 29)
4. Miracle of feeding 5000 and Day of Decision (April, 29)

III. Ministry outside of Galilee (April, 29, to April, 30)
1. Probably Pentecost (in Jerusalem . . . June, 29)
2. Journey to northern Galilee (June to October, 29)
3. Feast of the Tabernacles (October, 29)
4. From then to the Feast of Dedication (October to December, 29)
5. Dedication (December, 29)
6. From then to withdrawal to Ephrem (December, 29 to March, 30)
7. Last journey to Jerusalem (April, 30)
8. Ministry in Jerusalem (April, 30)
   a) Sunday: procession of palms
   b) Monday: cursing of fig tree
   c) Tuesday: debates and eschatological discourse

This outline roots the principal events of Christ's life in time and place. It is important at the outset to stress two facts: Christ's life on earth was human and it was, therefore, real; and it ended in failure.

The fact that Christ's life was real means that all His preaching and miracles were not so much sham. Jesus of Nazareth was not merely apparently human. We may not realistically argue that God, had He wished, could have given the grace of conversion to all those Pharisees and Sadducees who opposed Christ. Followed out logically, this would mean that Christ's disputations with them were just so many words. It would mean that He was not totally absorbed in His work, since, had He wanted, He could have convinced all of them. As a result of such a way of thinking, Jesus of Nazareth is made so divine that He is less than human. His preaching, for example, becomes just so much marking time until He can get down to the real work of salvation — that is, to His passion-resurrection-ascension.

Two more examples bring out the point. When he said, "Come back and be my follower" to the rich young man, He truly offered an invitation (Mt 19:16–26 and parallels). Again, Jesus of Nazareth strove to impede Judas' betrayal. How Christ can effectively extend an invitation and then give only sufficient grace to have that offer accepted and all of this not be a contradiction, we do not know because it is the mystery of His grace. This much is certain. There is no contradiction, no more than between God's will for universal salvation and sin. Both exist. Christ wished to save the men of His day. He spent Himself unsparingly for this end. Unless Jesus of Nazareth was serious in His everyday acts, His life becomes mere play-acting.

Once it is admitted that Christ's life was real, that He drained Himself to convert, the conclusion is inevitable: Jesus of Nazareth was a failure. You might hasten to object, "Impossible! He saved mankind." Agreed! But the facts of the Gospel are clear. He preached, He worked miracles, and He asked for faith. On the whole His hearers rejected His preaching, ignored His miracles, and refused faith. The mental suffering of Christ cannot be appreciated until the full extent of His failure is measured and understood. Only then do we begin to understand His humanity.

Now let us return to the above outline. Jesus of Nazareth began the proclamation of the Kingdom with some miracles in order to make Himself known. After a few months, He changed His style and gave a discourse, the Sermon on the Mount, a type of preaching in which He presented His demands on the Jews in simple but profound language. Its simplicity could be understood by the most rustic. Its profundity would attract the most spiritual and learned. He hoped therefore to capture all as He preached throughout His land. After about six months of this style of preaching, He turned to parables. Why?

A parable explains only if the key is available. If not, it only stirs curiosity and provokes meditative chewing. Christ gave the key only to the few who asked Him. Why, then, did He use parables? He realized the people were refusing His direct teaching. It was too much for them to accept the perfecting of the Mosaic Law by a miracle-working carpenter. Thus He gave them some more months to think about His teaching. In other words, He expressed the same teaching on the Kingdom in a form that would be intellectually enticing.

The emphasis on the parabolic way of teaching continued for about six months. A short period of the most striking of miracles followed. He then asked the people to choose or to reject Him. The day had to come. He had postponed it until the people had more opportunity to be disposed for the decision. The culmination of His public ministry of miracles and preaching had come; Jesus asked that the people believe in Him. Whether He meant, historically speaking, "Believe in Me as a divine person" or "Believe in Me as Messiah" we cannot know; but one thing seems to us certain: the miracle of the feeding of the 5000 provided a public showdown. The people rejected Jesus and His claims.

Disputes, disbelief, rejection were the answer. The rejection was so final and complete that our Lord asked the Twelve, "Are you, too, minded to go away?" (Jn 6:67.) They chose to remain and so began the sojourn around the environs of Tyre and Sidon. Jesus devoted the time to the Twelve, preparing them instead of preaching to the people as a whole. He had failed.

Once the people had shown their unwillingness to follow Him, Jesus was doomed. The leaders could now safely dispose of this potential troublemaker. Many were still loyal, but a general insurrection, if He were killed, was no longer to be feared. Crucifixion was the answer to this failure.

We will see in the following almost all of the above in much greater detail. From this overview, you have a peg for dates and places of events in Jesus' life. More important, you know Jesus as a sincere human who battled to avoid His human failure.

2. *Crucify Yourself*

The imprisoning of John the Baptist was the providentially assigned signal for Christ to begin His own public ministry in earnest. And when Jesus began, He required the whole of man wholly. In Chapters 5 to 7, St. Matthew has captured the simple profundity of the Nazarene's exacting demands.

The Sermon on the Mount couches the loftiest truths in the most simple terms. One example must suffice: "Look at the birds of the air: they do not sow, or reap, or store up provisions in barns, and yet your heavenly Father feeds them! Are you not more precious than they? And which of you can by fretting add one minute to his span of life?" (Mt 6:26 f.) The most ignorant have seen birds. He knows their utter dependence. Yet they succeed in living. This is due to God. Through such a comparison, everyone can understand Jesus' teaching on the value God places on man. But more is taught. The most profound philosopher could not delve into the mysteries of premotion upon which predestination rests and understand it; yet in these three sentences such a mystery is taught.

This is but one sample. Every one of the many sayings gathered together in the Sermon on the Mount is as lividly clear and as fathomlessly wise. Our Lord was casting down the gauntlet of His discipleship. The Galilean Carpenter demanded the most radical loyalty. To His disciples, it is true, He promised happiness. This is the keynote of those who would be called Christians, "Blessed are the poor, blessed are the meek. . . ." And blessed means happiness.

Christian happiness arises from unstinting dedication to God. To see the requirements Jesus laid upon those who would follow Him, study the following outline as you read Matthew 5–7:

I. The Spirit of the Kingdom: beatitudes (Mt 5:3–12).

II. Social requirements of our Lord's disciples: They must be the salt and the light (Mt 5:13–16).

III. A comparison between the New Law and the Old.
   1. The principle: the Old was good; the New is perfect (Mt 5:17–20).
   2. Application of the principle: to anger, chastity, etc. (Mt 5:21–48).

IV. Interior spirit of His disciples.
   1. Principle: God must be the motive (Mt 6:1).
   2. Application to almsgiving, prayer, fasting (Mt 6:2–18).

V. Attitude toward material goods.
   1. Principle of detachment (Mt 6:19–21).
   2. Necessity of detachment (Mt 6:22–24).
   3. Examples from nature (Mt 6:25–34).

VI. Rules of conduct about charity, discretion, confident prayers, discernment of spirits, rule of obedience (Mt 7).

Our Lord was demanding the most radical loyalty to God's will. Never could one be a Christian and merely a giver of money or a faster or a praying man. The motive of doing it only to please God would have to be there. Never could a Christian be one who refrained from murder but became angered. No Christian, the one who lusted in his heart. "Be perfect, then, as your heavenly Father is perfect" (Mt 5:48). The challenge was then, even as it is now, excruciatingly exacting. "Love the Lord your God with your whole heart, and with your whole soul, and with your whole mind" (Mt 22:37). Paul rightly interpreted this as a holocaust, a total offering to God (Rom 12:1–3).

3. Why Parables?

The Sermon on the Mount required a man wholly. We have seen it summarized in the word "love." Another paraphrase is, "He who loses his life for my sake will find it." Perhaps the best précis is, "And he who does not take up his cross and follow me is not worthy of me." The Jews knew from example what a crucifixion meant. Small wonder that they could not surrender themselves to such a demand.

The leaders first realized what He expected. Yes, such preaching undermined the law-keeping Pharisees. For them, perfection was in the external minding of the Law. The aristocratic Sadducees realized that their clung-to riches would be out of place in such a religion. If the people succumbed to this new teaching, their power would be overthrown. And the chiefs of Judaism united in their opposition. St. Mark capsuled this animosity in four brief but pointed steps. The enmity of the Pharisees and Sadducees crescendoes from silent criticism (Mk 2:1–12), through the questioning of the disciples (2:13–17), to challenging Jesus (2:18–28), and ends in a death plot (3:1–6). This tension mounted over months. But opposition was always present.

Jesus must have seen not only the leaders but also the people turning from Him. Some became enemies quickly. Others remained indifferent. For these latter, miracles were worked. During the months of July to November, as He preached the Sermon again and again, He saw the reactions in the people. How would they respond if now called upon to choose for or against the Galilean? Would they choose for Him? Jesus decided to delay their choice. He chose to teach less clearly so that they would still be interested, but could muse over His sayings.

And the period of the parabolic teaching began. Jesus' mercy had found a way to stave off their decision.

What is a parable? A parable is a literary or oratorical form in which a fictitious but plausible narrative teaches one and only one point. That point must be given by the author of the parable. A riddle is much the same. One who doesn't compose it, or learn the solution from someone who knows it, is not certain of the riddle's meaning. The hearer is teased to guess the answer. He is not sure of it until the composer puts all the enigmatic parts together. In a parable too, the meaning must be given. Once given, the narrative part of the parable becomes an easy way to remember the teaching.

Why did Christ change from the clear teaching as in the Sermon on the Mount to parables? His parables were essentially an act of mercy. There were three groups of people listening to His sermons: the well-disposed, His enemies, and the many who were vacillating. The well-disposed could easily attach themselves to the immediate disciples and learn the inner meaning of the parables. His resolute enemies had come only to spy and would take nothing from His sermons.

The parables were directed especially at the vacillating. Their hesitancy was not a case of grave sin against Jesus' message. It was rather an attitude almost forced upon them by the prestige of the hostile scribes and doctors.

For such men the parabolic teaching did not demand, as did the Sermon on the Mount, an immediate decision. The undecided were sent back to await a more favorable season, and were not excluded from the Kingdom of God.

How the people must have asked each other, "What did the carpenter mean by 'The Kingdom of heaven is like a mustard seed'? What indeed did the Master signify by 'The Kingdom of heaven is like a sower who sowed seed on the wayside, on rocky ground, and on good earth? How is the Kingdom of heaven like a pearl of great price? How is it like leaven? How is God's Kingdom like a net with good and bad fish in it?' " (Mt 13.)

Jesus' mercy had found a way to delay decision. The people's curiosity was excited. Some would have the humility to ask Him or His immediate followers what was meant. Others would not yet have to choose between crucifixion and giving Him up. All would have another few months to mull over the Sermon on the Mount and the parables.

4. *Day of Decision*

The Day of Decision was near. If the people were ever to be convinced, now was the time. Jesus increased His miracles. It was a time of crisis. An individual was insufficient. Help was needed. The Twelve must aid. Thus, "After calling the twelve apostles together one day, he gave them power and authority — authority over all the demons and power to cure diseases. He then sent them out to preach the kingdom of God and heal the sick" (Lk 9:1 f.).

Between December, A.D. 28 and April, A.D. 29, Jesus Himself worked striking wonders. He calmed the storm. He sent the legion into the swine. He cured Jairus' daughter. He publicly stopped a woman's hemorrhage (Mk 4:35–5:43).

And one day in April, A.D. 29, the Day of Decision had come. Jesus' preparation for it was grandiose. He fed 5000. He walked on the waters of the Sea of Galilee. The stage was well set. From the multiplication of the loaves and fishes, the crowd knew that here was a miracle-worker. They wanted Him for their king. And He refused this (Jn 6:1–21).

Not to be turned aside, the crowd followed. "How did He cross without a boat?" And Jesus came directly to the point. "You are looking for me, not because you saw manifestations of power, but because you partook of the loaves and made a hearty meal of them" (Jn 6:26). "What you want is a circus. You want easy bread. You want to be amused and fed without working." And then Jesus asked them clearly to accept Him as a worker of divine signs.

The full significance of Jesus' words were not understood. This much, however, was: this man was exacting full loyalty to Himself. And the Jews openly wrangled (Jn 6:41). Some said He could be followed without question. Others said that a man who was demanding such wholehearted obedience must be rejected, "He is only the carpenter!"

On the one hand, do not belittle the demand made by Jesus. He asked for total submission to Himself, who was — to them — no more than the village carpenter. On the other hand His mercy had planned and provided for the Day of Decision: He had taught plainly in the Sermon. He had given them about four additional months of parabolic teachings and striking miracles. Now He asked for loyal trust.

And He allowed no doubt about the demand. He said it, rephrased it, and repeated Himself many times. John has given the account in his sixth chapter and perhaps has made it even more explicit. But this much is certain, the Jews had no doubt that He was demanding a unique submission.

About 2000 years of Jewish history was being resolved that day near the Sea of Galilee. Abraham, Moses, David, Isaiah — all had awaited that day. When the providential moment of time came, the response was, "Such language is hard to bear; who can listen to it?" (Jn 6:60.)

Remember what had been said about the sincerity of Jesus of Nazareth. In this pitched battle, He was not idly sitting in a tent. Granted that His divine knowledge was there and thus He did know the outcome, His human nature was fighting to win these people and He lost. One author has expressed it, "His first year of work ended in utter failure."

And the rout was so complete that He had to ask the Twelve if they too were lost to Him. Could they continue giving full subservience to Him when they knew that total love was what He intended to require? The question must have pierced Him to the quick, even the need to ask it, "Are you, too, minded to go away?" (Jn 6:67.)

The people wished a political and explosive Messiah, one who would work miracles like Jesus worked, but more regally. They wished a Messiah who would give them food. Yes, it has been well said, "A circus and a circus performer." As long as He did these things, He could be their king. When He required total giving on their part, they went away. He asked them to believe Him and all He taught. It was too much — at least for them.

5. *Victory Through Defeat*

But for the Twelve not too much has been asked. Jesus had asked complete confidence. And this confidence would be tried soon, even more than it had been on that fatal Day of Decision. The Jews expected a national hero as their Messiah, one who would restore all the grandeur of the Davidic Kingdom and more. Jesus revealed that the true Messiah would suffer and die before entering glory. An unsettling paradox was this. In these four months He would teach that triumph came through defeat, glory through disgrace, joy through suffering, power through weakness, resurrection after death.

In July, A.D. 29, Jesus asked for an open confession from the Twelve, "Who do you say that I am?" Peter confessed Jesus to be the Messiah. And, in turn, Jesus revealed the mystery of the ages. He allowed them to glimpse the true messianic work, "From that time on Jesus began to make plain to his disciples that it was necessary for him to go to Jerusalem, suffer much at the hands of the elders, high priests, and Scribes, be put to death, and on the third day rise again" (Mt 16:21). For the Jewish Apostles, what an unexpected revelation! His own people, the Apostles' teachers and leaders, would make the Messiah suffer! He would suffer in the very city of Jewish triumph, Jerusalem! He would be put to death! Peter's reaction voiced all of their thoughts, "May God spare you, Lord, this must never happen to you!" (Mt 16:22.)

And yet, instead of denying it or correcting their misunderstanding, Jesus said that they too must accompany Him, "If anyone wants to become my follower, he must renounce himself and shoulder his cross; then he may be a follower of mine" (Mt 16:24). This was required of the Messiah's disciples: to be nailed to a cross.

What a turn of events had come about! They had confessed Him to be the Messiah, Savior of the people. And He, while telling them they were right, prophesied a passion and death before glory. He promised them the very same. The Apostles were human. Did they therefore not think of leaving Him? If Peter chided Him for being mistaken, did not the Twelve huddle and discuss what He could mean? Would the Day of Decision of the crowd at the Sea of Galilee be again repeated, "Such language is hard to bear; who can listen to it?"

Three of the Twelve had their faith strengthened. "Six days later, Jesus took with him Peter, James, and the latter's brother John, and led them up a high hill for the sake of privacy. Here he changed his appearance before their eyes" (Mt 17:1 f.). What a joy to know that ultimate triumph

was assured to Him and to them. The Father was with Him.
Moses and Elijah were there. They had an assurance that
they and He would be victorious.

Jesus' teaching about Himself as the Messiah was the all-
important instruction in these months He devoted to the
disciples. He would explain how important was their future
messianic ministry since even one soul was value enough to
rejoice heaven. What charity, humility, and zeal must the
leaders of such a soul have (Mt 18)! But they could never
forget the prophecy of salvation through suffering for both
the Messiah and His followers.

6. *Jesus of Nazareth, the Wonderful*

In April, A.D. 30, Jesus arrived in Jerusalem. The procession of palms signaled His death. The crowds had previously
rejected Him on His own terms. And, since the rulers did
not know that He would never accept the people's type of
kingship, they saw in Him only an enemy capable of foment-
ing insurrection. Rome might then remove all their power.
The Sanhedrin might come to an end. With people and rulers
against Him, He must die.

On the following Tuesday, the debate of all time took
place. Jesus answered the seemingly insoluble dilemmas of
tribute to Caesar, resurrection, greatest command, and His
own authority. He countered by making the leaders stumble
on how the Messiah could be both David's Lord and David's
son (Mk 11:27–33; 12:1–40).

His final days are known to all. The Last Supper with its
perpetual gift of His historical self in the Eucharist and His
sacrificing self in the priesthood preceded His captivity. The
clots of blood falling from His body in Gethsemani testify
to His psychological sufferings (Lk 22:44). Sleeplessness and
scourging prepared His body for death. Crucifixion with its
mortal asphyxia caused His death.

If this were the end of Jesus, He would deserve our compassion. But He rose. The early Church in its hymns, preach-

ing, earliest creeds, and Gospel commemorated His victory over death, sin, and Satan. He rose in power to make converts where He had failed in His earthly life. He ascended to give us the power of God unto holiness, to give us God's Spirit.

This victory through failure ends our treatment of the life of Christ. We have concentrated only on Jesus' sincerity and consequent failure. For the piety of each of us, the failure of Jesus is the most consoling of lessons. For the happiness of each of us, His resurrection is our guarantee that our failures too can be turned into victory.

The life of Christ remains a wonder for the oldest as well as for the youngest Christian. He is a wonder never sated, no matter how long nor how deeply pursued. He is the wonder of a child opening a Christmas present. He is the wonder of a scientist discovering the nucleus of the atom. He is the ceaseless wonder of a life that says, "It is not over, but living. 'I live, and you, too, shall live' (Jn 14:19). 'My Lord and my God!' " (Jn 20:29.)

CHAPTER TEN

THE WORD OF SALVATION:
THE GOSPELS

1. *The Literary Form of "Gospel"*

THE Gospels are the only reliable, written source of the life
of Christ which we possess. But the Gospels do much more
than depict Christ's life on earth. Each evangelist has used
Jesus' message and His life to teach a special side of the
Good News proclaimed by the Savior.

One of the most obvious proofs that the evangelists were
not writing merely a biography of Jesus is that they say almost
nothing of the first thirty years of His life.

A more general indication of the lack of biographical
interest is the curious changing of the same material in the
first three Gospels (called the Synoptic Gospels). We will
see an example of this in greater detail later. Right now, we
cite a simple example. Matthew says, "The rebels, who had
been crucified with him, insulted him in the same way" (Mt
27:44). Luke, on the other hand, says that one of the robbers
insulted Jesus but the other asked forgiveness and was saved
(Lk 23:39–43). This is only one example. The entire Gospel
tradition is based on this curious mutual divergence. If the
evangelists wished to write a biography, they would never
have permitted such obivous discrepancies while using the
same traditions.

In this section we will see an explanation of the similarity
in both content and form of the first three Gospels. The
following sections treat more fully the differences of the
Synoptics. This combination — (1) similar preexisting traditions and (2) individual use thereof — to tell the joyful news
of salvation is called the literary form of "Gospel." As we

shall see later, John's traditional material is so distinct as to provide no difficulty.

After almost one hundred and fifty years of trying to solve the mutual relation of the Synoptics, called "The Synoptic Question," scholars are not in accord. The most widely accepted explanation today is that Matthew's and Luke's works used the same sources, one of which was Mark's Gospel. The sources were the following: (1) oral traditions of what Jesus said and did; (2) a Greek translation of an Aramaic work containing some statements of Jesus; (3) Mark's Gospel.

This would explain the mutual relationship of the material found in the first three Gospels. But scholars also noticed that there was a great similarity in many of the literary forms. We have already seen the parable (p. 102 f.). Each of the Gospels has many parables. You know that each Gospel contains a passion account. But the Gospels also have many stories about Jesus' miracles and many of Jesus' declarations.

The so-called miracle stories follow a set plan in Matthew, Mark, and Luke. The circumstances, the wonder itself, and the effect produced are normally successively described. You can find some illustrations in Mark 1:23–38; 4:35–40; 6:45–52.

Jesus' declarations also follow a form which is identical in the first three Gospels. Everything in the account has been subordinated to some statement of Jesus. Examples of His pronouncements on various Christian practices are: Mark 10:13–16; 12:41–44.

We have given only a few examples of the pronouncement stories and miracle stories. Add to these the passion account and you will see why scholars fit a good part of the first three Gospels into one or another of these forms. Thus the first three Gospels are very similar both as to matter and form.

Yet there are striking differences in the use of this matter. As mentioned, Luke says that one of the robbers was sorry. Matthew says that they both derided Christ. How can this discrepancy be explained? The evangelists were not writing a biography or even writing history *for the sake of history*. Their purposes varied. They were using the life of Christ to explain, teach, console: Mark, to encourage the Roman Church; Luke, to teach the universality of salvation; Matthew, to present Jesus as the new Lawgiver and King. We shall see this in greater detail in the following sections. The point to keep in mind now is that each of the evangelists used the traditional material of the community in his own way, and for a determined purpose, a purpose inspired by the Holy Spirit.

You may be wondering whether such an explanation ruins the history of the Gospels. Far from it, the history of the Gospels is solid. All agree that the Synoptics rest on a prior tradition. Moreover, the forms listed above are forms a community would employ to carry its message (pronouncement stories) or to remove the scandal of the crucifixion of its founder (passion narrative), or, last, to show that He should be accepted (miracle stories). Thus the evangelists are using the forms handed down from the very earliest years after Christ and maintained by the community of His followers, the Church. The witness is therefore a community's testimony, not an individual's. We have an historical nucleus that Jesus lived, founded a Church, died, and rose. Perhaps we shall never know whether some of their details really happened or not, e.g., did a man ask forgiveness on the cross? The certainty of the essence of Christ's life is without doubt.

And we have really gained by the evangelists' use of the community tradition. We have gained because under the inspiration of the Holy Spirit, we have Mark's Jesus to console, Matthew's Jesus to teach, and Luke's Jesus, our Savior.

The Gospels are the only written, reliable source of Jesus' life and they give us a solid core of the life, work, death, and resurrection of Jesus. Written for men who believe, they also tell us the enchanting figure of a Consoler, a Teacher, a Savior, and in John, our Way, Truth, and Life.

2. *Jesus Reveals God's Will to All*

This section introduces you to Matthew's Gospel. The date, purpose, author, and audience will be presented. A summary of its teachings, manifestation of Jewish opposition, and passion account will be given.

Written sometime between A.D. 70 and 80, the first canonical Gospel was destined for Jewish readers — both converted to Christianity and not. The Greek Gospel is certainly the inspired word of God; it is based on several sources, as we saw on page 111, one of which is most likely an Aramaic Version. The author of the Greek is unknown. He wrote to show that Jesus was the fulfillment of God's promises: the King and the Kingdom of the Savior have come.

God's King and Kingdom summarize Matthew's teaching. The King is the promised Davidic Ruler, the fulfillment of the promises to Abraham (Mt 1 and 2; cf. pp. 121 ff.). God's kingdom is not joined by adhering to a human and political society, but by accepting God's revealed will.

The King, Jesus, had the right to reveal God's will; only He, the Son, knew it (Mt 11:25-27). He could disclose God's will because He had God's authority, "The Son of Man has authority over the Sabbath" (12:8). Lastly, Jesus could manifest God's will because He showed the sign and mercy promised by Isaiah (12:15-21) and because salvation is only in Him (14:13-36).

What then is God's will, God's revelation? Matthew's Gospel presents it in five blocks of doctrine that would have immediate significance for a Jewish audience, for implicit throughout is a comparison of Jesus with Moses: (1) the Sermon on the Mount (Mt 5-7) gives its spirit: dedication, internal and external, to God (cf. above, p. 101 f.); (2) Matthew 10 contains the marching orders for Christian convert-makers: nothing useless, total commitment, and single-mindedness; (3) in Matthew 13, one aspect of the Kingdom is described in parables: an external union, a Church which will spread; (4) Chapter 18 specifies the union of the members of the Church: one family, they must avoid scandal and forgive an erring member; (5) Matthew 24 and 25 detail the fall of Jerusalem and foretell the end of the world, teaching: victory to the persevering and punishment to the wicked.

In summary, these five doctrinal sections teach that the Christian himself, internally dedicated to God (cf. also 15:1–20), must convert others, even the Gentiles (15:21–16:12) to God's Kingdom, God's family, as he awaits the final days. This teaching is found in Jesus' Church. And this Church is founded on the rock, the man with the keys, the master of the beast of burden: Peter (16:13–20). Jesus' disciples must be willing to follow Him, even to the cross (16:21–28), which will bring ultimate triumph (17:1–26).

Chapters 19–23 contain further details of God's will: divorce, clung-to wealth, and obstinate rejection of Jesus — all keep men from God's marriage feast. "For many are called but few are chosen" (22:14). And during Jesus' life, the leaders had contemptuously refused His call. Mt 8:1–9:34 detail many of Jesus' miracles in the presence of the Pharisees, who judged, "He is a tool of the archdemon; that is how he drives out demons!" (9:33 f.)

Matthew's passion account describes the sufferings of Jesus, God's spokesman, and the rejection of Him as the Promised of Israel. His resurrection is the victory of the King and assures the same to the citizens of His Kingdom (Mt 26–28).

Matthew's Gospel has been partially summarized in 23:37:

> Jerusalem, Jerusalem!
> Murderess of prophets!
> Stoner of the messengers sent to you!
> How often have I been willing
> to gather your children
> as a mother bird gathers her brood
> under her wings!
> But you refused it!
> Mark well: you will find your house

> abandoned — a prey to desolation. Yes,
> I tell you, you will not see me again
> till you cry out: "A blessing on him
> who comes in the name of the Lord!"

The rest of Matthew's teaching can be summarized by saying, "But my Kingdom whose children need me, to whom I give my will, whose rulers are divinely sealed, and to whom I shall give eternal happiness is always open to you and to all, if only you would say, 'Blessed am I, your God!' "

Matthew's Gospel was meant primarily for Jews. Its teachings of God's will are relevant for us Christians today. Its teaching, that Jesus is King and the Revealer of God's will, will be relevant for eternity.

3. *Jesus, the Son of God, Was Misunderstood and Persecuted Too*

Divine yet perfectly human, misunderstood yet always loving — this was Jesus, the Christ, the Son of God whom Mark presented to the persecuted Roman Christians.

Mark told this story with all the vigor, candor, sensitivity, and simplicity of a ten-year-old. He had a message which he couldn't contain. His frequent "and's" are the tool normal to an excited child. He breathlessly reports his account, and this vividness paints an unforgettable picture of the human Jesus.

The author of the second canonical Gospel is the John Mark of Acts 13:5. A disciple of Paul, he was too timorous to follow Paul's difficult journeys and turned back (Acts 13:13; 15:37–40). Perhaps Mark's sensitivity accounts for the enthusiasm of his Gospel.

Dated between A.D. 63 and 70, Mark's Gospel is the earliest of the canonical Gospels. Whatever the precise date, Mark's message is the most primitive both in mode of presentation and in development of doctrine. Mark's unpolished presentation of the human Jesus is a most precious stone in the mosaic of the Gospel picture.

From the wealth of doctrine on the kingdom of God (4:1–35, etc.); the value of a soul (9:41–47), true greatness (10:35–45); prayer (11:20–25); faith (*ibid.*); reward (9:40); and marriage (10:1–12), we will choose Mark's three most outstanding concepts: Jesus was (1) the Son of God; (2) not understood as the true Messiah; (3) as human as any man who ever lived.

Jesus, the Son of God, has the divine power. He works miracles of healing (1:29–31; 1:40–45; 2:1–21; etc.). Power over water and over storms is His (4:35–40; 6:45–52). Devils obey His rebuke (1:23–28; 1:32–34; 3:20–30; 5:1–20).

Jesus is the Son of God and the Messiah. But the true significance of His messianic character was not perceived while He lived. Time and again Jesus forbids the divulging of who He is. The devils (1:34; 3:12), the cured (1:44; 5:43; 7:36; 8:26), the disciples (8:30 and 9:9) are forbidden to reveal the Christ. Why this caution? The reason is that Jesus was being misunderstood. The devils and the cured would have broadcast that a wonder-worker, not a savior from sin, had come. The people expected a marvel-worker; Jesus came to save their souls. Even Peter did not properly apprehend the meaning of the Messiahship (8:33). It is true that Jesus rises, but His manifestation will not come about until the end of time (16:8 — N.B. 16:8 ends Mark's Gospel; 16:9–20 is an inspired addition to it, not fitting with Mark's style, vocabulary, or teaching).

The misunderstood Messiah and the Son of God are two of Mark's chief teachings. When he paints a picture of Jesus of Nazareth, Mark seems most at home. His true exuberance can tell of the Son of Man, the Man by excellence. Yes, Jesus it was who didn't know who touched Him when the lady of the hemorrhage had been cured (5:30). Jesus was ignorant of the Day of the Last Judgment (13:32). And the Man was not only deficient in knowledge but also in ability. He could not work miracles in Nazareth (6:5).

If in describing Jesus' intellect and will, Mark is daring, how much more so in his picture of the Man's affections. More than once the Apostles had to chide, to scold, to admonish Him. He slept as they almost drowned (4:38). Peter told Him that He would never suffer (8:32). The disciples had to tell Him how much money would be needed to buy bread for His hearers (6:37 f.).

It is true that frequently He is merciful and charitable. Compassion brought on the miracle of the loaves and fishes (6:34). Charitably He ate with public sinners (2:13–17). But, not less often, Mark tells that He was angry, grieved, indignant (1:41, Greek text; 3:5) and sighed deeply at misunderstanding (8:12).

Of all the many sides of this portrait, Mark has painted most beautifully His tenderness toward children. He insists on food for the twelve-year-old risen girl (5:43). He blesses the children, takes them in His arms, and uses their "Give me" as an example that adults might beg the Kingdom (10:13–16).

The human, hidden Messiah, Son of God, was to be an inspiration to the persecuted Romans. In A.D. 64 the persecutions of Nero broke out. What more important message to buoy them up? Jesus was human enough to feel sleepy, hungry, deep sorrow (the Passion, especially the Agony in the Garden), but to act charitably even to His own disciple-betrayer (13:26). Just as Jesus was misunderstood as Messiah, so the Roman Christians are misunderstood by their persecutors. Just as Jesus' glory awaits ultimate triumph in His second coming, so too the persecuted Romans will achieve glory through disgrace and death. The Romans, human beings, have the human Jesus who was the Son of God, guaranteeing their glory.

Truly, wrote Mark:

It was necessary for the Son of Man to suffer much. . . . If anyone wants to be my follower, he must renounce himself and shoulder his cross; then he may be a follower of mine. Why, he who would

save his life shall lose it; but he who freely parts with his life for
the sake of the gospel will save it in the end (8:31–34 f.).

Mark's message is as relevant today as then.

4. *Salvation Through Jesus by the Spirit*

The joyful news of salvation is told by Luke in two separate books: the Gospel according to St. Luke, and the Acts
of the Apostles. In the former, Luke's primary interest is to
show that salvation is in Jesus. In the latter, Luke shows how
God's spirit spread salvation "even to the very ends of the
earth" (Acts 1:8).

A sixth-century tradition which makes Luke a painter may
be too late to be creditable. But he is an artist with words.
He depicts personalities who will remain ever alive. The Good
Samaritan, the Pharisee and Publican, the "Prodigal" Son are
all found only in his Gospel.

A psychologist has called St. Luke a man who was the
composite of two great Francises. He had the joy of the
Assissian and the meekness and love of De Sales.

Writing between A.D. 70 and 80, Luke sends the good
news of salvation to Gentiles. In this message of salvation to
Gentiles and Jewish refusal, Luke gives us many of Jesus'
teachings. Joy, prayer, and charity are among the most
graphic.

The keynote of the good news of salvation is joy, blessed-
ness. "Blessed are you poor" (6:20; cf. 6:17–45). The notion
of the peace of being blessed occurs again and again in Luke
(10:23; 11:28; 12:37; 14:15). Luke tells his readers to be
confident even in persecution and suffering (12:4–40). And
Luke's nearly final verse tells how the disciples "in a trans-
port of joy retraced their steps to Jerusalem" (24:52).

Indeed, the news of salvation is joyful. For Luke, it is
also prayerful. Jesus prays (6:12; 10:21 f.; 22:39–46). Persevere in prayer as a woman pestering a venal judge (18:1–
8). Prayer must be humble, without the "I-trouble" of the

Pharisee (18:9–14). It should be, "Father may you be known and glorified . . ." (11:1–13).

Love — charity — is present in Luke's Sermon, "Love your enemies; treat kindly those that hate you" (6:27; cf. 6:27–38). The example of the Good Samaritan teaches that any and all should be recipient of kindness (10:25–37). And the delightful description of the visit of the Lord to Mary and Martha teaches that the Lord must always be the one loved (10:38–42).

Joy, prayer, and love are taught by Luke. But most important is his message that redemption is here. His first two chapters depict salvation's dawn (cf. pp. 121 ff. below). Salvation from devils (4:33–44) and from death itself (8:40–56; 7:11–17) is at hand. Freedom for sinners has come (5:32; 7:36–50).

Three example stories of the Lost Sheep, the Lost Coin, and the Lost Son are ageless proof of God's forgiving, solicitous love for man. His love for the sinner is so strong that it seeks out the lost, as a shepherd who searches, finds, and joyfully embraces the one out of the hundred who had strayed (15:1–7). God's longing for the sinner's conversion is like a woman who sweeps the house to find a lost coin — trifling in itself, but a treasure to her and, when found, a cause of delight to her (15:8–10). Most of all, God's desire for a sinner's return is as generous, forgiving, embracing, anxious — loving — as a father toward a son who was lost. The father rushes to the son, interrupts his speech of contrition, clothes him as his son, and scolds the small-minded, scandalized elder brother (15:11–32).

Salvation was proferred by God, but Jesus' countrymen, despite miracles, had refused it (5:18–26; 6:6–11; 11:14–26; 19:11–28; etc.). Zacchaeus (19:1–10) and the thief on the cross had accepted it: "I assure you, this very day you will be with me in paradise" (23:43).

Christ's redemptive act brought salvation. The Acts of the Apostles relates the expansion of the joyful news of man's deliverance from sin. The Lord had promised, "You shall be my witness in Jerusalem and in all Judea and Samaria and even to the very ends of the earth" (Acts 1:8).

Almost every chapter of Acts teaches that in bringing about salvation, God's power — God's spirit — is at work. Under the spirit, the word spread from tiny Jerusalem (Acts 1:1–8:3) to the Samaritans (8:4–25), to all of Judea (8:40). Asia Minor and Europe soon have their communities of Christians (13:1–28:31).

Luke's heroes have their interesting tales of conquest. Peter told the fearsome Sanhedrin he was obeying God (5:17–42). The Lystrans thought that Paul was a god (Acts 14:10). Philip converted the treasurer of Ethiopia's queen (8:26–40).

There were also times of trial and peril. Christ's stalwart emissaries were threatened with extinction: Peter was imprisoned (ch. 12). Stephen, martyred (chs. 6 and 7); James, killed (12:2); Paul tasted death often (9:22–25; 13:50; 14:5–19; 19:23–40; etc.).

The budding Church was itself in the throes of conflict. A unity so perfect as that of Christ's Church (cf. 2:42–46 and 3:32–37) had its Hellenist and its Jewish factions nevertheless (cf. 6:1–11). Doctrine given by God seemed to contradict doctrine given by God. How know which was right? Men asked, "Is circumcision necessary for salvation?" Peter stated the Christian dogma, "We believe that we are saved through the grace of the Lord Jesus!" (15:11.)

Externally the Church encountered opposition. The Greeks could not understand a resurrection (17:32). The Jews opposed this sect which called them murderers (2:36; 21; etc.). The Romans were confused and as yet undecided (22–24).

And yet in all the tribulations told in the Acts, the teaching of joyful salvation is loudly proclaimed. For Christ conquers and is unconquerable. Who are His enemies? Gamaliel, Paul, death, shipwreck? They will succumb. Who must be won? Jews? By the thousands! Gentiles? By the nations and territories! Even in pagan Rome itself, Christ was invincibly proclaimed by the intrepid missionary Paul. Though in prison, Paul preached unhindered — for how could Christ be enchained?

Salvation is here. It is ours. Luke depicts it. Only in Jesus is there salvation!

5. *Dawn of the Promised Salvation — the Infancy Narratives*

The enchantment of the Nativity accounts of Matthew and Luke has held Christians spellbound for these twenty centuries. All of us know the descriptions of the Annunciation of John and of Jesus, the births of both, the visit of the Magi. Less known is that both Matthew and Luke teach profound theological truths in their Nativity accounts.

For Luke, the birth of Christ was the beginning of the fulfillment of the messianic promises. He teaches this fulfillment in a theological progression which begins with a description of the Precursor's fitness and ends with the Messiah's first words.

John was born in the most sublime of Old Testament circumstances. He was promised by God's angel to a priest offering at the highest cultic moment. He was born of a barren woman (like Sarah, Samson's mother, and Samuel's mother). John himself would dispose the Jews for Christ. A fit precursor for Jesus was John!

The Child given to Mary who personified those loyal to God (the "Remnant") will be the Holy One, the King, fulfilling the promises of God. Mary's response to this Annunciation is to praise God in her *Magnificat* for fulfilling His promises to the needy. All of these events are steps toward the final entrance of the Child Jesus into the Temple.

Three more steps must intervene. The joy of the Remnant over the marvel of who the Precursor will be (1:57–59) and greater marvel at the birth of the Messiah, Jesus, which means "Yahweh saves" (for "Yahweh," cf. Appendix). The presen-

tation of the Savior begins the work of the further purification of the Remnant. The last step in Luke's dynamic theology
is the first recorded word of Jesus, "I must be about the
things of my Father" (2:49; author's translation). Jesus,
standing in the temple, chooses to do the will of God His
Father. Salvation's dawn!

In Chapters 1 and 2, Luke teaches the dawn of salvation
as the Lord Jesus chooses to do God's will. Matthew's first
two chapters teach that the Old Testament was fulfilled in
the circumstances of the birth and infancy of Jesus. According to Matthew's genealogy, Jesus is the Messiah, descendant of King David and the Patriarch Abraham. The
child is the "Emmanuel" of Isaiah 7:14. He is born in David's
town, as Micah predicted. Rejected by the Jews (2:1), he
is nevertheless acknowledged king by the Gentile Magi. As
Hosea had foretold, the son is brought out of the land of
slavery.

The very killing of the Innocents shows Israel's looking for
the Savior and yet rejecting the Savior who was already in
the world. Finally, the Nazarene would be the promised of
Abraham. For Matthew, therefore, Jesus is the Emmanuel,
born of a virgin in Bethlehem, adored by Gentiles, and called
from Egypt. He is the cause of sorrows and yet the offspring
of David who would eventually save His people.

All our explanation about Chapters 1 and 2 in both Luke
and Matthew must have raised the question, "Is this explanation an exegesis of the literal sense or just an accommodation?" Remember the literal sense is that meant by both
author and God. We believe the above exposé of the infancy
accounts of Matthew and Luke is their literal sense.

A man of faith under the guidance of the Holy Spirit,
Matthew, looked upon the historical facts of the birth of
Christ and compared them to the Old Testament. From his
meditation on both, he came up with new and deeper truths
concerning the birth of a child: faith believes that this child
fulfilled the Old Testament. Faith also accepts that this child

was King, was Messiah. Faith shows the Gentiles accepting Him and the Jews rejecting Him.

Luke, a man of faith, taught as Matthew. Luke's own background in letters was most likely much more schoolish than Matthew's. As a result, his use of the Old Testament in the first two chapters is much more subtle. But, as Father Laurentin has shown, there is hardly a verse in these first two chapters that does not have a more or less direct allusion to the Old Testament. Some are clear, some are nebulous (cf. Laurentin: *La Theologie de S. Luc I et II*).

In the more scholarly jargon of the Scripture scholar, what Matthew and Luke have used is a midrashic literary form (cf. p. 9). From their Old Testament-based meditations on the historical facts of the birth of Jesus, they have realized the sublime truths listed above. Only faith can see them. Scripture, after all, is primarily meant for men of faith, not for historians.

It is hard, not to say impossible, for us to be satisfied with this statement. Children of a materialistic era, we wish to know the uncolored fact. How many of us have not thought, "All right, did Matthew and Luke write history or not? Get to the point!" The question, as we shall see, is more easily asked than answered. The point, and this is the point, is the divine truth which faith tells us is there. What we mean in this last sentence, if we may use an example, is this. Say what you will, the virginity of Mary cannot be proved. Only faith can give it the "aye" or "nay." And this virginity is far more important than whether Mary ever asked, "How can this happen since I know not man?"

But the historian continues to urge, "Did it happen or not?" Before we can answer that, we must discuss what is meant by the word "history." The lowest common denominator for a "definition" of history is this description: history is something that happened. No two people's portrayal of this "something" will be the same. Let us take an example. Buy two papers tomorrow. Each paper will tell that the president held a conference, let us suppose. The author of one of the paper's articles is a Republican. He begins his portrayal of the fact, "Looking tired after an arduous session in cabinet, the (Democratic) president tried to solve these difficulties." The other writer, a Democrat, reports, "Smilingly, the president dispatched all queries." You will ask, "Well, what is the history?" The fact is that the president answered some questions at a press conference.

The purpose of the example was to show that no one writes an uncolored history, except a statistician. Every author interprets the event, the "something that happened." The Christians, Matthew and Luke, interpreted the events of Christ's birth in the light of faith — a faith nourished by the Old Testament. The truth they came forth with is founded on faith, and it is true because the faith is true.

Their inspired teaching about salvation is the prime interest. Was everything they built this teaching on a statistic? "Did the angel appear to Mary? Did the Magi come? What about the star? How many children were massacred?" The fundamental historical facts of the annunciation and birth of Jesus of Nazareth are without question. Father Stanley summarizes the only sane Catholic view at the present time when he says: "In writing midrashic stories, they [the rabbis] freely introduced details found in scriptural passages so that where [as here, Matthew's infancy narratives] a single version of incidents has survived it is next to impossible to discern the historical nucleus which always forms the basis of such stories" (*New Testament Reading Guide,* #4, p. 10).

When we do not know, let us admit it. On the other hand, do not think that any article of the faith is in jeopardy. Our faith is based on proofs of credibility all together different from whether or not we will ever know how many feathers were on the wings of Gabriel as he appeared to Mary. And this notion does introduce the only real answer that at present can be given to those who are honestly seeking to know, "Did the Magi come? Did an angel appear?" The answer is,

"What is the difference?" The teaching of Matthew and Luke is true: The Gentiles accepted the Messiah. Mary is the Mother of God. Jesus did begin the salvation of mankind. These are the truths meant by Matthew and Luke. And you know, they were far closer to reality than we would be if we knew that there was a miraculous star. Curiosity would be slaked. Would faith be deepened?

6. A Sample of the Beauty and Inspiring Qualities of the Synoptic Gospels

We have seen in general that the Gospels are both sources of the life of Christ and also literary works in their own right. In this section, we will view the miracle of the paralytic found in Mark 2:1–12, Matthew 9:1–8, and Luke 5:17–26 from both aspects. What, in other words, did this miracle mean in the life of our Lord? What did Mark, Matthew, and Luke mean by it in their Gospels?

In our Lord's own life, the miracle showed His divine powers. His words were enough to cure a paralyzed man. He added to this healing power the claim to do an act which only God could do. He claimed to forgive sins. One who could work a miracle after such a claim must be at least God's representative. Jesus of Nazareth was showing His listeners that God was with Him. The miracle showed His mercy and love for the believing sick man.

The incident also shows the ill will of the Pharisees who witnessed it and accused our Lord of blasphemy. The people's amazement is underscored and shows the crowd who would seek Him for His wonders and later His free bread — but never to give themselves to Him. The miracle, paradoxically, is a preparation for His crucifixion.

We have already explained that the evangelists used the traditional stories about Jesus to teach something pertinent to the early Church. What did Mark teach by this combination miracle and pronouncement story (cf. p. 111)? The pronouncement is in Mark 2:10, "Now I want you to understand that the Son of Man has power here on earth to forgive sins." The miracle is best summarized in verse 12, "He rose and, taking up his mat, walked out before the eyes of all."

This pronouncement and miracle story is one of a series of stories which shows the swelling hatred of the leaders of the Jews toward Jesus (cf. p. 103). What a lesson for the Roman Church which was about to undergo persecution. Jesus, before them, had been judged a blasphemer (2:1–12). Jesus had had His disciples questioned (2:13–17). Jesus had Himself been challenged (2:18–28) and His enemies had united in a death plot (3:1–6). Yes, the Roman Christian Church could take heart at Jesus' example. The man with power to forgive sins and cure a paralytic was judged a blasphemer!

The teaching that Jesus was blasphemed by His enemies is the heart of Mark's message of consolation and encouragement in this passage. Many, many other teachings can be found in it. In fact, every word could bring out some shade of encouragement.

Matthew's teaching is a little more subtle than was Mark's. To understand it, we must bear in mind two principles. The first is that the crowd's reaction is an important part of a miracle story (cf. p. 111). The second is that Matthew is a Christian writing to many who already knew Christian doctrine.

From these principles we deduce the first of Matthew's teaching. This inspired teaching is that humans can forgive sin. Note well we did not say, "a human," but "humans." Using Mark as a source, Matthew changes Mark's "All were enraptured and praised God with the words: 'Never did we see the like!'" (Mk 2:12) to: "As the crowds saw this, a feeling of awe came over them, and they praised God who had given such power to *men*" (Mt 9:8). The logical deduction would have been "who had given such power to *man* [i.e., to Jesus]." Matthew says "to men." Christians could easily see in this a reminder of the sacrament of Penance.

Matthew has added a second teaching, that the claim of

Christianity is based on the Messiah's (Jesus') miraculous powers. This teaching is far more subtle since it is learned only by linking verse 8 with the entire story of the paralytic. Our minds would have taught it otherwise. The Jews, weighing each word, would have united them and made the teaching the totality of the pericope. Men forgive sins because the Man had worked miracles.

Matthew also teaches the divinity of Christ. The Jewish leaders suggest the true principle that only God can forgive sins. Jesus, reading their minds (9:4), asks, "Which is easier to say, 'Your sins are now forgiven,' or to say, 'Rise, and walk?'" (9:5.) The obvious answer is that it is easier to say, "Your sins are forgiven," because no one can tell if that happened or not. Since both claims are based on divine power, if Jesus does the harder (that is, the visible) and claims to do the secret one, He can also do the other: forgive sins. He is God on both counts.

Luke teaches two points by the same story: the Gentiles should not be scandalized by the Jewish leaders' refusal to accept Jesus; and the sacrament of Penance is not so impossible of belief.

Surely for the Gentiles at the time of Luke the fact that the leaders of the Jews themselves had rejected the awaited Messiah must have been a scandal. Luke answered this scandal by saying that Jesus' activity was the power of God among the Jews to save them (Lk 5:17).

Luke also teaches, "We have seen extraordinary things today" (5:26). From 5:12 to 6:11 Luke is teaching that there is now a new order perfecting the old though at variance with the leaders of the latter. Luke includes 5:17–26 to show that the sacrament of Penance is not impossible. "Yes," the Gentile could say after reading about this marvelous miracle, "the power of forgiving sins is not such as to keep me from being a Christian. We have seen extraordinary things today." In other words, since the Son of Man had forgiven sins, perhaps He had given that power to His official representatives.

Luke thereby dispels the scandal of the Jewish leaders' rejection of Jesus. Jesus had come to save them from their sins and they had refused Him. Anyone, seeing the wonderful things of miraculous cures and forgiveness of sins, should have been converted. Certainly an opportunity for others to forgive sins is at least implied. This is especially true since the forgiveness of sin would be in keeping with Luke's general teaching of universal salvation.

Each Synoptic has described the same incident in Jesus' life. Each has turned that incident slightly to give a particular teaching. His teaching is God's word to us. It is God who teaches through Mark's miracle story that Jesus was blasphemed. It is God who teaches through Matthew that there is a sacrament of Penance. It is God who teaches through Luke that we should not be scandalized at a claim to forgive sin once the Man had forgiven them; let us rather be thankful for the chance at salvation.

7. *Jesus, God, Gives the Divine Life*

St. John wrote his Gospel sometime between A.D. 90 and 100. Then an elderly man and mystic, he had been a fellow laborer with Jesus of Nazareth, God. One of the three intimates within the Twelve, he was the disciple "whom Jesus loved." By trade he was a fisherman. By temperament he was a "son of thunder" who could ask for the place of highest dignity, demand that fire be called down on unfriendly towns, and forbid that a nondisciple work miracles.

John's audience consisted primarily of devout and thoughtful persons. He wrote for Jews and Greeks, for Christians and non-Christians. According to the reader's piety and ability, he would understand the Gospel of John.

Why did John write? In 20:31, John says, "This much, however, has been recorded that you may persevere in your belief that Jesus is the Messiah, the Son of God, and that, through your belief, you may have life in his name." He wrote to give life.

What did he write? Take notions you encounter at every moment of every day, transform them to the divine, and bring them thus transformed back to man. Of these John wrote. All of us know the reality meant by bread, life, light, a word, the vine, the way, the truth. John's Gospel tells us that Jesus is the reality which these words denote. John's Gospel teaches that we may participate in the reality which is life, light, the truth, etc. "And of his fullness we have all received a share — yes, grace succeeding grace" (1:16). Jesus of Nazareth, the Eternal Word (i.e., the Logos), bestows on him a participation in the divine reality (1:1–18).

In his Book of Signs (2:1–12:50), John follows a general pattern of giving a sign and the theological meaning of it. A sign is more than a miracle. On the one hand, it represents a comparable Reality in God. On the other hand, it looks to the act of redemption by which Jesus earned a participation of that divine reality for man. The Cana miracle is a sign of the messianic new times when Jesus gives His blood to replace the old covenant (2:1–11). The miracle of healing the son of the royal official and the miracle of the pool of Bethsaida prepare John for his teaching on the Life-giving Word (4:42–5:47). The multiplication of the loaves in Chapter 6 is the sign of the Bread of Life who is Jesus. In 9:1– 10:42, sight given to a man born blind is a sign of the Light-giving Word. Jesus gives divine knowledge, actual graces to understand, and divine wisdom to appreciate the divine truths. Lazarus' miracle in Chapter 11 is a sign of Jesus, the Word-giving Life.

Interspersed throughout 2:1–12:50 are other theological teachings without a preceding miracle. In 3:1–36, John teaches that Jesus brings a baptism which gives man the divine nature. By the incident of the Samaritan at Jacob's well, Jesus is presented as the Logos-Redeemer, who brings the divine life to all, enabling man to worship God (4:1–42). In Chapters 7 and 8, John manifests Jesus as the Word, the Life-Light who was rejected by the Israelites.

From Chapter 13 to 20:31, John gives the Book of the Passion. Perhaps the most profound message ever written by man is found in John 13:1–17:26. Every word is of the deepest theological weight:

Chapter 13: Having loved His own, He gave them an example of humility and charity that they too might be humble and sacrifice themselves for Him.

Chapter 14: Confidence: (1) in Him who prepares a place in heaven for those who love Him; (2) in Him who sends the Comforter to plead for us; (3) in Him who dwells with the Father and Third Person in His lovers. "Peace is my legacy to you" (14:27).

Chapter 15:1–17: Christ lives in His disciples who must love Him and His. "I am the real vine . . . you are the branches. . . . Love one another" (15:1, 5, 17).

Chapters 15:18–16:33: The disciples are assured of victory, even in the midst of persecutions, for their Lawyer is the Third Person, "Have courage, I have overcome the world" (16:33).

Chapter 17:1–26: Christ's prayer effects the unity of believers with one another and to Himself, "Just Father . . . may the love with which you love me dwell in them as I dwell in them myself" (17:25 f.).

In 18–20, the Passion itself is related. In general it tells the crucifixion of Jesus. But for John this too is a theological event of the highest reality: it is Jesus who is King; Jesus, who, in being pierced, is causing the divine nature to be given to us through Baptism and the Eucharist.

Chapter 21 is an inspired addition to John's Gospel. It has a beautiful story giving a timeless lesson for us: the disciple is powerless without the Master; with Him he can do all (21:1–14); the Supreme Shepherd must die for the flock (21:15–19).

The contemplative John has told us who is this Word, not in a theological treatise, but in historical encounters. Jesus is the Life, Light, Savior for us who believe in His name.

CHAPTER ELEVEN

THE WORD TO THE GENTILES

1. *Paul to the Thessalonians: Be Holy While You Await Christ's Certain Coming*

"THIS man is my chosen instrument to carry my name among nations and their kings and among the children of Israel as well" (Acts 9:15).

How had God prepared His choice to convert nations? By birth, God made Paul a Roman Jew. By temperament, God readied a fiery heart. By intellectual endowment, God fashioned him a genius. By education, God formed a rigoristic lawyer. By conversion, God re-created Saul of Tarsus as Paul of the Gentiles.

Paul's epistles to his Gentile converts were not written as theological treatises. As occasion required, he wrote. He was questioned and he answered. There was some problem and he sent forth his solution. They are priceless for their teachings on the Christian life. We will briefly summarize them in this and the following sections.

The first epistles that he wrote were to the Thessalonians. Acts 17:1–15 describes Paul's stay in Thessalonica and the consequent persecution. His friend and frequent companion, Timothy, brought news that Paul's converts remained steadfast. But Timothy also brought the alarming news that some vices and certain doubts about the dead had begun.

At the beginning of A.D. 52 Paul wrote his first Epistle to the Thessalonians. He rejoices that their virtue continued even in suffering. He tells them not to be disturbed about the dead. Christ's second coming in glory (the Parousia) will bless

both living and dead. Paul expected the second coming soon,
it seems. He taught, and this is what is inspired, that the
proper attitude for a Christian was confident watching. Christ
would come. Be armed with Christian virtues when He comes
(1 Thes 4:13–5:11). "We do not want you ignorant concerning those who are asleep, lest you should grieve, even
as the rest who have no hope" (1 Thes 4:13).

For one awaiting Christ, the vices that were reported
among the Thessalonians were out of place. Chastity, piety,
diligence were the proper Christian attitude (1 Thes 4:1–12).
"What God wills is your sanctification" (1 Thes 4:3).

But matters did not completely subside in Thessalonica.
False preachers came teaching that the Parousia was at hand.
Paul wrote again somewhat later in the same year. He told
his readers that the telltale signs about which they had been
taught, especially the antichrist, had not yet come. How then
could they think the Parousia was as yet at hand? Paul did
not go into great detail about the antichrist. He simply summarized what they already knew: the antichrist's nature is
sin; his destiny is hell; his character is consummate pride;
and he is being restrained. The important point is that the
Parousia is not yet around the corner. Thus the Thessalonians
must continue watchful and clothed in the virtues of a Christian (2 Thes 2:3–12). "You brothers must not grow tired
of doing good" (2 Thes 3:13).

2. *Paul to the Corinthians: God Has Made Me His Fit
   Minister to Teach That Christ Is the Solution to
   Problems of Factions, Immorality, Idols, and the
   Resurrection!*

About the end of A.D. 51, Paul arrived in Corinth. He had
just before suffered heartbreak. One of his most erudite sermons failed (Acts 17:16–34). He failed because he appealed
to Christ risen. Then, as never before, he realized that Christ
crucified — foolishness to the Greeks and a stumbling block
to the Jew — was God's wisdom. In his first epistle to the

Corinthians, written some five years afterward, we have the profound summary of what Paul learned from his failure. He compares the wisdom of God and the wisdom of man, 1:17–3:4.

In addition to Paul's teaching of God's wisdom, he solved some practical problems existing in Corinth. Some doubted if they would rise from the dead. Factions divided them. There was a report of incest. Christian arraigned his brother. Jealousy accompanied the celebration of the Eucharist.

Paul answered all these problems on the basis of the unity of Christians to one another and to Christ. The unity was similar to that of the human body (1 Cor 12–14).

Since Christ had risen, the Corinthians — one with Him — must also rise (1 Cor 15). Factions destroyed the unity in Christ (1 Cor 1:10–4:21). Incest and sinful intercourse was to make Christ the member of a harlot (1 Cor 6:15; cf. 5:1–6:20). No two Christians should go to court. This would be to seek what was already theirs in the unity in Christ (1 Cor 6:1–11 and ch. 13). The jealousy before the Eucharist brought on early death (1 Cor 11:17–34).

Another question very important to page converts bothered the Corinthians. "May we eat meat offered to idols?" Paul responded that since an idol was nothing, such meat could be eaten. Eating idol meat was licit — unless a less wise Christian would be thereby led to sin. Then, just as Paul had relinquished some of his privileges, this right too must be foregone. Idol offerings were nothing, not idol banquets. Banquets were considered to unite partakers to the idol. A Christian united to one another and to Christ by and in the Eucharist could not banquet with the devil of the idol banquet. In sum, "Whether you eat or drink, or do anything else, do all for the glory of God" (1 Cor 10:31; cf. 1 Cor 8:1–11:1).

Another problem was present. The new converts were seemingly scandalized by pagan debauchery. They began wondering if marriage itself was good. Paul taught that intercourse in marriage was good and that virginity was better.

"It is better to marry than to be on fire with passion" (1 Cor 7:9; cf. 7:1–40).

Practical difficulties but profound solutions. Paul could have done no other way. He regarded the unity of Christian life as an act of God's wisdom. He regarded it as being united to Christ and to one another.

A few months after Paul had sent his epistle, Titus brought back news that not all went well. True, there had been an improvement subsequent to Paul's previous letter. But a new group which questioned Paul's authority had arrived. These false apostles dispirited and disquieted the young Church.

In his second epistle to the Corinthians, as in no other epistle, Paul lays bare his heart. It pleads his case. The Corinthians are written on his heart (1 Cor 3:2). Therefore what letter or recommendation does he need? But they have forced him to give his credentials. So let it be! His right and authority are from God. As Apostle, he can command (2 Cor 3:1–5:10). Having preached a crucified Christ to them, Paul had sought nothing for himself (2 Cor 5:11–6:10). Forced to boast of himself, who can compare with his titles, his works, sufferings, and extraordinary gifts? (2 Cor 10:1–13:13.)

In the midst of this fiery polemic, Paul is mindful of the money needed in Jerusalem. He beseeches the Corinthians to finish the collection (2 Cor 8:1–9:15). Let them give generously, "For God loves a cheerful giver" (2 Cor 9:8).

To the Corinthians, Paul set down his rights to preach and teach. He taught "Christ and him crucified" (1 Cor 2:2).

3. *Paul to the Galatians and Romans: The Just Man Lives by Loyalty to God, Not by the Jewish Law*

The second Epistle to the Corinthians exposed Paul's heart. The Epistle to the Galatians, probably written in A.D. 57, unleashed his just anger. Agitators had come to Galatia. They taught that the Jewish Law was necessary for salvation. They undermined Paul by denying that he was an apostle. And Paul's own converts in Galatia were being taken in!

Paul's answer? "Paul, an Apostle, not one commissioned by man, nor by any group of men but one appointed by Christ and God the Father . . ." (Gal 1:1). Without letup, the Apostle to the Gentiles claims his right to teach (Gal 1:11–2:21; 6:11–18).

And his teaching is that the Jewish Law is void (Gal 2:21; 3:19–29). The Crucified took upon Himself the curse that the Law brought upon man (Gal 3:1–14). The promised offspring of Abraham (Gal 3:15–18), Jesus Christ, gained the right for His own to cry, "Abba, Father" (Gal 4:1–7). As Christians and sons of God, the Galatians are free from subservience of the Law (Gal 4:8–31).

Nailed to the cross with Christ (Gal 2:20), a Christian must practice His virtues (Gal 3:12; 5:1–6:10). In one sentence, Paul to the Galatians: "God forbid that I should glory except in the cross of our Lord Jesus Christ" (Gal 6:14).

The epistle to the Galatians was an impassioned plea for faith — i.e., loyalty based on knowledge of who Christ is. The epistle to the Romans, written about the same time as Galatians, is a closely reasoned, profound exposé of the same thesis. Paul was writing to a group who did not know him. And he was writing for them to accept him and aid him in his proposed journey to Spain (Rom 15:23).

Paul explains to the Roman Christians what Christianity was for him, knowing thereby that they would accept him. His credentials are that justification and consequent glorification come only from Christ.

Justification is not to be found in the sins of the Gentiles which merit the wrath of God (Rom 1:18–32). Observing the Jewish Law does not sanctify (Rom 2:1–3:20). Rather, "They are sanctified freely by His grace through the redemption which is in Christ Jesus" (Rom 3:25). In Chapter 4, Paul confirms his teaching on holiness from the Old Testament.

Next, Paul laid down before the Romans his belief that

justification must result in glorification. God's love for us
gives hope. Human love is strong enough to die for a friend.
God's love was strong enough to die for an enemy. Now as
friends, a justified man has an assured hope of glory (Rom
5:1–11).

Glory must result from sanctity. Christ died to sin and
rose to glory, overcoming the thralldom of the Law (Rom 5:
20–7:25). Therefore we may hope. Still, man's weakness
tries to undermine his strength (Rom 7:13–25). Therefore
we fear. How to resolve the tension between hope and fear?
The reasons for hope are surer. God's power unto holiness
(the holy spirit), God's adoption of us, the Third Person
and Christ — all are for us (Rom 8:1–39). In one sentence,
justification must terminate in heaven's glory because, "If
God is for us, who is against us?" (Rom 8:32.)

God's love in Jesus Christ gives us justification. We are
assured of ultimate glory. But can one not object that in
sacred history God was unwise in His original choice of
Israel? No, God could choose whom He willed. Israel had
to be rejected because of its sins. Instead of doubting God's
wisdom, let us hymn a praise to it shown in His choice,
punishment, and bringing even sin to manifest His wisdom,
"Oh the depth of the riches and of the wisdom and of the
knowledge of God!" (Rom 11:33; cf. 9:1–11:36.)

To such love and wisdom, man must respond. The only
response is a total gift of self, a holocaust by love (Rom
12:1–3, 8 f.). Paul enumerates the Christian virtues in
Chapters 13–15 and concludes, "May God, the source of
hope, fill you with all joy and peace based on faith, that you
may abound in hope by the power of the Holy Spirit" (Rom
15:13).

Paul tried to hold for Christ the Galatian converts. He
quietly exposed to his Roman Christians his belief. To both
the Galatians and the Romans he taught, through the epistles,
that a just man lives by unwaivering loyalty to God.

4. *Paul to the Colossians and Ephesians: Jesus of Nazareth, the Unique and Awesome Mediator, Redeemed His Body Who You Are*

Paul went to jail in Rome from A.D. 61–63 (Acts 21:17–28:31). Most likely word then reached him that two heresies were being spread in Colossae. One of these was that between God and man there were beings who had to be worshiped (Col 1:19; 2.8 f., 20). The other was that certain superstitious rites had to be observed for man to be saved (Col 2:16, 21 ff.).

Paul dispels both errors by showing the fullness of being in Christ, the perfect and unique Mediator (Col 1:13–20). It follows that no other intermediary of salvation can exist. The so-called "philosophy," which taught intermediaries, is false and pernicious to Christ (Col 1:21–2:15). A Christian, one body (Col 2:19) with this Head, must practice Christ's virtues. The prescriptions of magical human dictates voids the new creation (Col 2:16–4:6). Paul says, "In him [Christ] is embodied and dwells the fullness of the Godhead. In union with him . . . you have been made complete" (Col 2:9 f.).

The Epistle to the Colossians emphasizes Christ, the Unique Son of God and Head of His Body. During his years in prison, Paul had time to meditate deeply on the Body. From this meditation stems the circular epistle to some churches in Asia Minor called the Epistle to the Ephesians. While a healthy doubt may be entertained whether St. Paul wrote this epistle, the better opinion is that he did. Its inspired teachings on the exalted dignity of a Christian remain whether Paul wrote it or not.

And its teachings are sublime. From sin to grace and from grace to glory — Ephesians proceeds. One with Christ, the Christian has an exalted place with Him before God (Eph 1:1–23). Pagan Christians have passed from deserving God's wrathful punishment to the glory of sharing in the resurrection of Christ (Eph 2:1–10). Formerly barbarians, Chris-

tians are now cocitizens with saints (Eph 2:11–22). To
God's wisdom and love shown in Christ and His Body, a
Christian must respond by striving for perfection (Eph 3:1–
21). This perfection is charity, purity, etc. (Eph 4:1–24).
The Christian must be girded with Christ's virtues to fight
sin which tempts him and his family (Eph 4:25–6:20). Yes,
the mystery of the ages has been revealed. It is God's wisdom
unfolding in the eon since creation: "The Gentiles are joint
heirs and fellow-members of the same Body" (Eph 3:6)
. . . "that you may be perfected and bring to realization
God's complement" (Eph 3:19).

5. Paul to the Philippians, to Philemon, to Timothy and Titus: Hail and Farewell

Of all Paul's epistles, five are most personal. With four of
them, this familiarity is understandable since they were written to individuals. The tone of intimacy in the fifth is explained by Paul's predilection for the community at Philippi.

The Philippians alone were permitted to help him with a
personal contribution (Phil 4:10–20). He deeply appreciated
their emissary, Epaphroditus, sent to lighten his imprisonment, probably that of A.D. 61–63 (Phil 2:25–30). Paul
was so close to his converts at Philippi that he told them of
his bitter sufferings. How difficult that even Christians had
turned against him (Phil 1:15). His captivity would be for
Christ's glory (Phil 1:12–26). He thanks God for their love,
humility, and steadfastness in the faith (Phil 1:3–11; 1:27–
2:18). And he sent his friends the gift of the hymn to the
victory of Jesus, "Be of the same mind as Christ Jesus, who,
though he is by nature God, did not consider his equality
with God a condition to be clung to, but emptied himself
by taking the nature of a slave. . . . This is why God has
exalted him . . ." (Phil 2:5–11, passim).

Paul's love for the Philippians is evident. His care for a
runaway slave, Onesimus, appears in his letter to Philemon.
With the astuteness of a charlatan, Paul begs for the life of

his fellow Christian. No word in this epistle is without undertones for Onesimus' benefit. Read the guile of, "I, Paul, an old man, and also at present a prisoner for Christ Jesus, plead with you for my child, whose father I became during my imprisonment" (Phlm 9 f.). Could Philemon refuse his imprisoned and aged father (19) the life of his son (8–10)?

To his friends at Philippi and to Philemon, Paul wished "Hail well!" Even more joyously than this did he greet his personal friends Timothy (cf. especially 2 Tim) and Titus (cf. Ti 1:4). And since they would "hail well" if their flocks increased in God's love, Paul's epistles to them are filled with his concern for the souls entrusted to their care.

These three epistles are easy to understand. There is something for everyone in them: bishops (1 Tim 3:1–7; Ti 1:5–9) and deacons (1 Tim 3:8–13). All must keep the traditions and avoid error (1 Tim 1:3–20; 3:14–4:16; Ti 1:10–16; 3:8–11; 2 Tim 2:2; 2:14–4:5) and remain disciplined (1 Tim 3:1–14; 5:1–6:2; 2 Tim 2:1–3:7). Salvation awaits (1 Tim 1:15 f; Ti 3:3–7; 2 Tim 2:8–13; 4:6–8).

Paul's expressions are filled with hope, "Woman's salvation is in childbearing, if she perseveres in faith and love and holiness and modesty" (1 Tim 2:15). . . . Our salvation is assured. If the chief sinner made it, we too can be confident, "Trustworthy and deserving of wholehearted acceptance is the saying, 'Christ Jesus came into the world to save sinners.' Of these, I [Paul] am at the head of the list . . ." (1 Tim 1:15) along with "For I am already on the point of being sacrificed; the time of my departure has come. I have fought the good fight, I have finished the course, I have kept the faith. What remains is the crown due to holiness which the Lord, the just Judge, will give me on that day, and not only to me but also those who love his brilliant coming" (2 Tim 4:6 f.).

Paul's second epistle to Timothy was his legacy. Paul foresaw his own death and wrote the "Farewell of the Apostle."

6. *Paul to Everyone: "The Breadth and Length and Height
and Depth of this Mystery, and to Know Christ's Love
. . ." (Eph 3:18 f.)*

A new enthusiasm and vitality had entered Paul's life one
day on the road to Damascus. His life had been transformed.
The new convert wanted to communicate his knowledge of
life's meaning. Others must know that they were "in Christ."
Paul wanted Christians to know that they lived in the place
(as it were) which is Christ. Saying the same thing in other
words, Christ and the Christians make one body. Thus
Christianity had to be meaningful, had to be lived and affect
everyday life!

There was an interdependence of Christ and Christians.
They needed Him. He needed them. They needed one another. Although Paul never used the word "mystical" to
qualify this bodily figure, we today call this union of inter-
dependent organized parts, the Mystical Body of Jesus Christ.

This being "in Christ" was one of Paul's principal ways of
explaining the meaning of life, one of his ways of answering
problems, and of presenting truths (1 Cor 12 and Rom 12).
Here we will consider Paul's teachings about the head and
members of Christ's Body.

For Paul, who was the Head of the Body? He was the
Jesus of whom the Gospel tradition witnessed. But Paul saw
Him as the Firstborn from the dead, the Creator-Redeemer,
the Cause of our resurrection, the Divine Emptiness who deserved the title of God even as did the Father (Col 1:15–20;
1 Cor 15; Rom 5:8 f.; 6:1–11; Phil 2:5–11; etc.).

For Paul, Jesus' crucifixion and resurrection, a single act,
effected the salvation of the members. The crucifixion was
God's wisdom even though it was a stumbling block for the
Jews and foolishness for the Gentiles (1 Cor 1). The resurrection made Jesus strong, capable of giving the divine life
to His members. "His Son . . . was constituted the *mighty*
Son of God by his resurrection from the dead" (Rom 1:4).

Who are the members of the body? To understand this fully, we must know who they were before His saving act. They were sinners without hope (Rom 7). Deserving the vengeful punishment of God (Rom 1:18–3:20), they were mired in the mud of Adam's sin (Rom 5:12). Weak, prone to sin, and sinners (1 Tim 1:13 ff.), of themselves they could do nothing toward justification (Gal 3:19–29; Rom 3:21–26).

Of such material, only a Head as Paul had described could make anything. And what did He make? Man is now a new creature (2 Cor 5:17). He is a creature with the earnest of salvation and heaven. He can already experience (if only he permits) the joys of the divine life (1 Cor 2:9 ff.; ch. 15; Rom 8:23–25; 5:1–11; 6:1–11). So certain is this hope of salvation that Paul realized after years of meditative study and teaching that it is a past event (Col 3:1–5). The Body *has* risen with the Head. Yes, Christians have "heaven on earth": joy, peace, patience, benignity, God's favor, etc. (Eph 4:1–6; 1 Cor 2:9 ff.; Gal 5:22–26, most of the salutations and endings of the Pauline epistles).

Sinners have now become saints. The old creature of Adam has given place to the new creation of Jesus. But this does not mean the Christian will not know suffering along with happiness. Paul is also a realist in the sufferings and tribulations of a Christian. For him the notions "tribulation" and "Christianity" connote one another. Sorrow is part of being a Christian (1 Thes 3:1–5; 2 Cor 11). Suffering is a corollary of being "in Christ." The members thereby fill up what is lacking in the sufferings of Christ for fellow members (Col 1:24 f.; 1 Cor 12:26).

The members are "saints." But this does not mean that they do not have to work out their own salvation. As Paul says, "Work out your salvation with fear and trembling" (Phil 2:12). The prime virtue is charity. The Christian must love the Crucified and His members (Rom 12:1–3; 1 Cor 13). To be "in Christ" requires obedience — the bend-

ing of the highest part of man, intellect and will, to another
man (Col 3:18 ff.; Rom 13). To be "in Christ" requires
purity lest they make Christ into a harlot (1 Cor 6:12–18).
Yes, for a Christian, constant giving is the measure of perfection — not *merely* the keeping of a set of laws. Paul, as
Jesus, required the whole man wholly.

On route to Damascus, the militant persecutor received
a new dimension in life. He learned that there existed a
union of people with a certain Jesus who had died for them
to give them the divine life. Paul's response was immediate
and wholehearted. Love must repay Jesus' own holocaust.
Suffering will perfect His body. Victory is assured "in Christ."
True for Paul, true for everyone! "In Christ" the human had
been re-created. God's wisdom had crucified His Son and
made Him rise in power. Through that Son and in that Son
Paul knew that God had given us already a surety of eternal
life.

CHAPTER TWELVE

THE WORD IN CHRISTIAN LIFE

1. *The Epistle to the Hebrews: Existence, Humdrum?*
   Let us Hasten to the Battles

LIFE is monotonous, tedious, boring? The Epistle to the Hebrews says, "No! Not a life which has a God for its Priest
and Victim. The vacuity of life has been filled by and with
Christ. Sufferings buy ultimate, splendid, everlasting victory!
'Let us hasten to the battles set before us looking to the
author and finisher of our faith, Jesus, who for the joy set
before him endured a cross' " (12:3).

The epistle's author is unknown. Arguments based on
style, vocabulary, and theological differences between this
epistle and those of Paul compound to argue against Pauline
authorship. Scholars disagree on both the audience and precise date (anything from A.D. 65 to 90) of Hebrews. The
literary form is more a sermon or an exhortation than an
epistle.

Whatever be the disagreements, the author of Hebrews
had a profound insight into Christianity and wished to give
that insight to his readers. He chose to impart this appreciation by preaching Jesus the Priest. His readers had lost sight
of Christianity. The humdrum living of everyday life caused
ennui. Relaxed in their pursuits of virtue, they forgot Christ.

In 1:1–4:13, the author tells them that they will have no
heaven if they forsake Christ. Jesus, the Unique Son of God,
is above angels and Moses. To Him must we listen. "God
. . . has spoken to us through his Son" (1:1) Through Him
alone may we enter into the promised rest: heaven.

Jesus, our Priest and Victim, will give heaven to those

who act on their faith in Him. From 4:14–10:18, the author sets down his profound teaching that Christ is a priest. Christ is greater than any Old Testament priest. He has instituted a covenant superior to that of Sinai. His blood, the sacrificial offering, uniquely remits sin. Because of Christ's saving act, the Christian lives in hope.

Let hope find expression in faithful acts — as others have lived in loyalty (10:19–13:17). "It is a dreadful thing to fall into the hands of the living God" (10:31). "Here indeed we have no lasting city; but we are in search of the city that is to come" (12:14). Jesus of Nazareth has set the example. He suffered and thereby entered into His own glory.

To see the connection between Jesus the Priest and the marriage bed takes faith. To be charitable because Jesus is at this moment offering His wounds in supplication requires loyalty. Hebrews teaches the connection. By faith and loyalty, by living as a Christian at every moment, humdrum life becomes exciting, joyful, and meritorious of eternity. "Let us hasten to the battles set before us looking to the author and finisher of our faith, Jesus, who for the joy set before him endured a cross" (12:3).

2. The Catholic Epistles — More Problems of the Infant Church

The Catholic epistles number seven, namely: James, 1 and 2 of St. Peter, 1, 2, 3 of John and Jude. Concerning five of these epistles the term "catholic" or "universal" is appropriate, since they are directed to a wide public. 2 and 3 John are meant for a particular group; they were titled "catholic," it seems, because they always accompanied the first epistle.

The Epistle of St. James. The author was James, the relative of our Lord, probably not James the Apostle. Written sometime between A.D. 45 and 60, this sermon exhorts Jewish converts to live as perfect Christians.

The epistle contains many practical enjoinders: "Faith without deeds is lifeless" (2:26; cf. 2:14–26). . . . "Human ingenuity is able to tame and has tamed every kind of wild beast and bird, reptile and sea animal; but no man can tame that restless evil, full of deadly poison, the tongue!" (3:7 f.; cf. 3:1–12.) . . . "Is anyone sick? He should call in the presbyters of the Church, and have them pray over him, while they anoint him with oil in the name of the Lord. . . . If he has committed sins, they will be forgiven him" (5:14 f.).

The First Epistle of St. Peter. The author of this epistle was St. Peter, Prince of the Apostles. Written about A.D. 63, the epistle was sent to persecuted Christians of Asia Minor. Its purpose was twofold: to comfort the persecuted and to encourage them in holiness. In 1:3–4:11, Peter seems to use a primitive baptismal liturgy to recall what holiness is and to give counsels for acquiring it. A baptized person, being one with Christ, must suffer as did Jesus (2:21–25; 3:17 f; 4:1 f.). The epistle ends with comforting words, "God, the source of all grace, who has called you to his eternal glory in Christ, will himself, after you have suffered a little while, perfect, steady, strengthen, and firmly establish you" (5:10).

The Second Epistle of St. Peter. The author claims to be Peter (1:1, 16–18; 3:1). Doubt that the author really is Peter arises from the religious and historical milieu presupposed by the epistle. It reflects a time after the first generation of Christians, that is, after Peter's death. Pseudonymity was a literary device common in the Old Testament. The Christians to whom the epistle was addressed knew that Peter died in A.D. 64 and that the epistle was written about A.D. 100. They therefore would have understood the *nom de plume* to mean that the epistle's teachings were to be accepted with authority. The author has summarized his instruction in 3:14, "Therefore beloved, since you await these events [those of the second coming of Christ, cf. 1:12–21; 3:1–18], make every effort to be spotless and blameless so that God may find you with a peaceful conscience."

The Epistles of St. John. Most likely the author of all

three epistles was the Beloved Disciple, the author of the Fourth Gospel. They were probably written between A.D. 70 and 90. All were sent to Asia Minor: the first to the group of churches near Ephesus; the second to one of these churches; and the third to an individual.

The thirteen verses which comprise the second epistle urge the Church to keep the faith against errors about the Incarnation. The third epistle thanks Gaius for the hospitality which he, unlike Diotrephes, had extended itinerant Christian preachers.

John wrote the first epistle to counteract errors about the divinity of Jesus and to teach Christians how to enjoy their union with God. John describes God as Light (1:5–2:27) and Love (4:7–5:12). In the same sections, he tells that a Christian shares in these attributes. In 2:28–4:6 God is described as Justice; man's virtue enables him to be holy.

For all of us who worry about a sinning friend, John wrote, "If anyone sees his brother committing sin that does not spell death, he should pray for that sinner and God will give the sinner life" (1 Jn 5:16). . . . For all of us, John wrote, "We know moreover that the Son of God has come and has given us understanding that we may know the True One. In fact we are incorporated into this True One, God's Son, Jesus Christ" (1 Jn 5:20).

The Epistle of St. Jude. Probably because the epistle is only twenty-five verses long, there are considerable doubts about its author, date, and audience. The best opinion is that Jude, a relative of Jesus, wrote it about A.D. 75 to a now unknown group. Jude wished to combat the errors of certain sinners who had recently come among his addresses. He gives examples of the punishment of sinners in the Old Testament and two apocryphal books. Sinners in New Testament times must learn from these examples that they too will be chastised. Verse 24 and the following nevertheless give encouragement to all, "To him then who is powerful enough to keep you from stumbling and to bring you blameless and exultant to the presence of his glory . . . belong . . . dominion."

The seven Catholic epistles show the problems of the infant Church. Many of the practical teachings are important for us. All of the words of encouragement and exhortation are needed by the Christianity of today.

CHAPTER THIRTEEN

THE APOCALYTIC WORD

The Struggle of the Victors: the Apocalypse

VICTORY is the keynote of Christianity. But by A.D. 100, persecutions were already raging. The persecutions were not of the petty variety, but of a grand scale by the all-powerful Roman Empire.

The dilemma of suffering and joy was not a new one for the Jew. When he returned from exile, he had been promised a glorious restoration and came back to broken city walls. As the Jew of that era had done (cf. p. 83), so now, John tried to console by appealing to God's past protection and love. John used the apocalyptic literary form.

His Apocalypse is not totally the same as, for instance, Daniel. John knew that the Christians' assurance of triumph was based on the already risen and victorious Jesus.

He told his message of victory in down-to-earth, concrete terms. For example, the Christians' struggle would be against such enemies as war, pestilence, strife, famine, earthquake, Satan, and so on. The Christians themselves were aided by prayer, endurance, Christ, the omniscient Father, and the fiery Holy Spirit.

John's terminology comes from a culture founded on the Old Testament, the Greek and Roman heritage, and early Christianity. Therefore, many of these concrete terms are today no longer used.

Even without the terminology equivalence, the *Apocalypse* can be read with profit by remembering: (1) prophecies are few, general, and of slight importance; (2) John wrote to solace and console. All of us wonder how God could permit wars, pestilences, Satan's rule seemingly to continue, the martyrdom of Christians, etc. Read John's answer: victory is ours, even though persecution will be ours.

Note well also, this message would not be accepted by a a man who does not believe in Christ. How tell such a man that he is victorious in Christ when all he can perceive is famine, war, hades, etc., on the earth? Only a man of faith sees the victory and knows that he has it now and will have it forever. Faith alone believes that Satan, sin, and death are already conquered and that Satan's sway is but for "a time, and times and half time" (12:14; symbol of the small quality of Satan's rule) as compared to the "thousand years" of Christ's reign (20:5; symbol of the great quality of Christ's rule). Sin can be forgiven. Satan's unlimited control over man is broken. Death will be overcome by resurrection. In these ways does the believer already taste victory.

John the poet and man of his own culture has written concretely and apocalyptically. He has written a message that we need in order to encourage us, just as much as the Christians of A.D. 100. It is a message of victory even though there are and will be struggles.

EPILOGUE TO PART TWO

THE WORD DWELLS AMONG US

"LISTEN! A Sower went out to sow. The Sower sows the word. And there are those who hear the word and welcome it; and they bear fruit thirtyfold. sixtyfold, or a hundredfold" (Mk 4:3, 14, 20; translation of *New English Bible*).

After this introduction, we hope that one thing is clear. God's word brings about its intended result. In creation, "God said, 'Let there be light,' and there was light" (Gn 1:3). God's word which made the covenant with Moses fructified into the "New covenant sealed with my [Christ's] blood" (1 Cor 11:25).

God admonished and threatened through the voice of the prophets. His word found its results in the punishment of the Exile. His word of consolation and hope was fulfilled in the messianic kingdom of Jesus of Nazareth.

The wise men queried the right way of living. God spoke in their quests. He answered His own questions in "Christ Jesus, who has become for us God-given wisdom and holiness and sanctification and redemption" (1 Cor 1:30). Truly,

> So shall my word be
>   that goes forth from my mouth;
> It shall not return to me void,
>   but shall do my will,
>   achieving the end for which I
>   sent it (Is 55:11).

But you too have at your disposal God's word. As you read the Bible, does the efficacy of God's word produce in you something that is over and above your mere dispositions at the time of reading? In other words, does the very act of reading the Bible produce, in and of itself, the effect — the grace — intended by God: that you love Him? This is presently a moot point in Catholic scholarship. If the answer is "yes" — and we incline to think that it must be — then we can hold that the Bible is akin to the sacraments. We can say that the efficacy of the Bible is the same as that of the sacraments, which, as we know, effect — i.e., convey — the grace they signify. We can speak of the Sacrament of the Bible. A towering concept!

Just as God's Word is present in the Eucharist awaiting only that man be not unwilling in order to make him holy, so, in the Sacred Scripture, the word become ink awaits only that man be not unwilling to read and to love:

> All Scripture is inspired by God and useful for teaching, for reproving, for correcting, for instructing in holiness, that the man of God may be perfect, fully equipped for every good deed (2 Tim 3:16 f.).

The word dwells among us.

APPENDIX

THE MEANING OF THE NAME "YAHWEH"

IN THE Confraternity translation of the Old Testament which we followed in this book, the Hebrew proper name for God, "Yahweh," has always been translated by "the Lord." We thought it best to follow the same translation in our book. Since the name is pregnant with theological meaning, however, we thought a word of explanation should be given.

The name "Yahweh" was probably revealed at the time of Moses (Ex 3:14). In Genesis 4:26, the Yahwistic (J.) source anticipated the revealing of the name.

The translation of Exodus 3:14 is disputed. All agree that no philosophical notion of being from one self is taught. Four general opinions can be found for the etymological significance of the name: (1) The root means "to fall or blow." The verb form is a Hebrew causative. Thus "Yahweh" would mean, "He who falls or causes to fall." (2) "He who causes to be," the Creator. (3) "He will be what he will be." The living God will guide history and will reveal Himself to His people continuously in their ever changing experiences. (4) The name is an exclamation of *"hu"* meaning "he" and *"Ya,"* meaning "oh," thus: "Oh, He!"

Whatever the etymology, the name was always used to teach that "Yahweh," the Lord, the God of Israel was able and willing to help Israel. Perhaps we could paraphrase Yahweh by "God with us." God had revealed His name, "Yahweh," to Israel as a guarantee of His mercy and help. History showed that the God of the Fathers had brought Israel out of Egypt. Yahweh was, and would continue to be, there to protect, to guard, to help, to admonish in order to achieve His salvation plan for Israel.

SELECTED BIBLIOGRAPHY

I. Modern Translations

The Holy Bible, New American Catholic Edition (containing the new Confraternity translation from the original languages for most of the books of the Old Testament). Various editions. A paperback edition, annotated by Rev. Joseph Grispino, was released in 1965 by the Guild Press for the Old Testament.

The Complete Bible: An American Translation by J. Smith, Edgar Goodspeed, and others, The University of Chicago Press, Chicago, 1948.

The Holy Bible in the Revised Standard Version. This is a revision of the King James Bible by American scholars. Published in 1952 it is available in many editions. In 1965 the New Testament of this version was approved for public use by Catholics in England.

The Anchor Bible. This is a multivolume project under the direction of W. F. Albright and D. N. Freedman. Catholic, Protestant, and Jewish scholars are collaborating in this enterprise, translating each book of the Bible afresh from the original languages, providing introductions, notes, and commentaries.

For the New Testament the following modern translations, made from the original Greek, are specially recommended:

The New Testament by James Kleist, S.J. and Joseph Lilly, C.M. The Bruce Publishing Co., Milwaukee, 1954.

The New Testament of the *New English Bible,* Thomas Nelson Sons, New York, 1962.

II. General Introduction

Dictionaries

Hartmann, L. (editor), *Encyclopedic Dictionary of the Bible,* a translation of the Dutch work of Van den Born, McGraw-Hill, New York, 1963.

McKenzie, John L., S.J., *Dictionary of the Bible,* The Bruce Publishing Co., Milwaukee, 1965.

General Introductions to the Bible

Bruns, J., *Hear His Voice Today,* Kenedy & Sons, New York, 1963.

Charlier, Dom Celestin, *The Christian Approach to the Bible,* Newman Press, Westminster, Md., 1957.

Hunt, Ignatius, *Understanding the Bible,* Sheed & Ward, New York, 1962.

Robert-Tricot, *Guide to the Bible,* two volumes, rev. ed., Desclée and Company, New York.

Vawter, Bruce, *The Bible in the Church,* Sheed & Ward, New York, 1958.

Wright and Fuller, *The Book of the God Who Acts*, Doubleday, Anchor, New York.

III. Subsidiary Sciences

Albright, W. F., *Archaeology of Palestine*, Pelican book of Penguin Books, Baltimore, Md., 1961.

—— *From Stone Age to Christianity* Doubleday, Anchor Books, Garden City, N. J., 1957.

Atlas of the Bible Lands, C. S. Hammond Co., Maplewood, N. J., 75 cents.

Baly, D., *The Geography of the Bible*, Harper, New York, 1957.

de Vaux, Roland, *Ancient Israel, Its Life and Institutions*, McGraw-Hill, New York, 1961.

Grollenberg, L., *Atlas of the Bible*, Nelson has published an abridged edition as well as an unabridged one.

Wright, G. E., *Biblical Archaeology*, Westminster Press, Philadelphia, Pa.

IV. Old Testament

History

Heinisch, P., *History of the Old Testament*, Liturgical Press, Collegeville, Minn., 1952.

Martin, D. W., *Guide to the Old Testament*, Vincentian Press, St. Louis, Mo., 1957.

Ricciotti, G., *The History of Israel*, two volumes, The Bruce Publishing Co., Milwaukee, 1955.

Introductions

Ellis, P. F., *Men and Message of the Old Testament*, Liturgical Press, Collegeville, Minn., 1962.

Moriarty, F., *Introducing the Old Testament*, The Bruce Publishing Co., Milwaukee, 1959.

Theology of the Old Testament

Gelin, *The Key Concepts of the Old Testament*, Sheed & Ward, New York, 1955.

Guillet, J., *Themes of the Bible*, Fides, Notre Dame, Ind., 1960.

McKenzie, J. L., *The Two-Edged Sword*, The Bruce Publishing Co., Milwaukee, 1956.

Commentaries or Notes on Individual Books

All books: Paulist Pamphlet Series on the Old Testament, Paulist Press, New York, 1961 (not yet completed). Liturgical Press series was begun in 1965.

Chaine, J., *God's Heralds*, Wagner, Inc., New York, 1955.

Hauret, C., *Beginnings, Genesis & Modern Science*, Priory Press, Dubuque, revised ed. 1964.

Kissaine, E., *Book of Isaiah*, Brown & Nolan, Dublin, 1960.

—— *Book of Psalms*, Westminster, Md., 1954.

Murphy, R., *Seven Books of Wisdom*, The Bruce Publishing Co., Milwaukee, 1960.

Vawter, B., *Path Through Genesis*, Sheed & Ward, New York, 1955.

───── *Conscience of Israel*, Sheed & Ward, New York, 1961.

Worden, T., *Psalms Are Christian Prayer*, Sheed & Ward, New York, 1961.

V. New Testament

Introduction

Wikenhauser, A., *New Testament Introduction*, Herder & Herder, New York, 1960.

Theology, Introduction

Ahern, B., *New Horizons*, Fides, Notre Dame, Ind., 1963.

Brown, R., *New Testament Essays*, The Bruce Publishing Co., Milwaukee, 1965.

Bultmann, R., *Theology of the New Testament*, two volumes, Scribner's, New York.

Dodd, C., *Introduction to the Fourth Gospel*, Cambridge University Press, Cambridge.

McKenzie, J., *The Power and the Wisdom*, The Bruce Publishing Co., Milwaukee, 1965.

Quesnell, Q., *This Good News*, The Bruce Publishing Co., Milwaukee, 1964.

Commentaries

Confraternity of Christian Doctrine Commentary on the New Testament, Catholic Biblical Association, 1942.

New Testament Reading Guide, Liturgical Press, Collegeville, Minn. (series of booklets on the New Testament).

Life of Christ

Fernandez, *The Life of Christ*, Newman Press, Westminster, Md., 1958.

Fillion, *The Life of Christ*, Herder, St. Louis, 1957.

Fouard, *The Christ, the Son of God*, Longmans, New York, 1944 (also available in paper book form).

Goodier, *The Public Life of Our Lord Jesus Christ*, Kenedy, New York, 1956.

Lagrange, M. J., *The Gospel of Jesus Christ*, Newman Press, Westminster, Md., 1938.

Prat, F., *Jesus Christ*, The Bruce Publishing Co., Milwaukee, one-volume edition, 1964.

Vawter, *The Four Gospels*, Our Sunday Visitor Press, Huntington, Ind., 1955.

Life of St. Paul

Brunot, Amedee, *Saint Paul and His Message*, Hawthorn Books, Vol. 70 of *Twentieth Century Encyclopedia of Catholicism*.

Holzner, J., *Paul of Tarsus*, B. Herder & Sons, St. Louis, 1945.
Knox, Ronald, *St. Paul's Gospel*, Sheed & Ward, New York, 1951.
Lapide, C., *The Personality of St. Paul*, St. Paul Editions, 1958.
Tricot, *St. Paul, the Apostle of the Gentiles*, B. Herder & Sons, St. Louis.

Theology of St. Paul
Montague, G., *Maturing in Christ*, The Bruce Publishing Co., Milwaukee, 1964.
Prat, F., *The Theology of St. Paul*, Newman Press, Westminster, Md., 1958.

VI. Magazines

Catholic Biblical Quarterly, a scholarly review from Catholic University of America, Cardinal Station 17, Washington, D. C.
The Bible Today, more popular, Liturgical Press, Collegeville, Minn.
Current Scripture Notes, very popular, short notes edited by Joseph Grispino and published by Alba House, Staten Island, New York.

SUBJECT INDEX

INDEX OF BIBLICAL REFERENCES

OLD TESTAMENT

NEW TESTAMENT